W9-DGP-972

Loving and Learning

James Kenny, Ph.D.

Loving and Learning:
A GUIDE TO
PRACTICAL PARENTING

ST. ANTHONY
MESSENGER
PRESS

CINCINNATI, OHIO

Nihil Obstat: Rev. Lawrence Landini, O.F.M.
Rev. Robert Hagedorn

Imprimi Potest: John Bok, O.F.M.
Provincial

Imprimatur: +James H. Garland, V.G.
Archdiocese of Cincinnati
March 13, 1992

The *nihil obstat* and *imprimatur* are a
declaration that a book is considered to be free
from doctrinal or moral error. It is not implied
that those who have granted the *nihil obstat* and
imprimatur agree with the contents, opinions or
statements expressed.

Scripture citations are taken from *The New
American Bible With Revised New Testament*,
copyright ©1986 by the Confraternity of
Christian Doctrine, and are used by permission.
All rights reserved.

The excerpt from *Dune*, by Frank Herbert,
copyright ©1987 by Frank Herbert, is reprinted
with permission of The Berkley Publishing
Group.

Cover and book design by Julie Lonneman
Cover photograph by Jim Whitmer

ISBN 0-86716-186-8

©1992, James Kenny
All rights reserved.

Published by St. Anthony Messenger Press
Printed in the U.S.A.

Contents

Introduction

The family is the oldest institution known, older than the Church, older than government and nations, as old as the first man and woman.

The family is in and of itself holy. When God chose to describe himself to us, he did not call himself a priest or bishop. Rather, he called himself "Father." God chose to identify with and to share his creative activities with the *family*. It is where new life is conceived in love. Within the family, that naive life is nurtured and nourished to self-sufficiency.

Supporting family relations may be the Church's most important task. In describing the God-life as that of a father and son, a parent and a child; in looking to the Holy Family as a model; in reverencing the beauty and sacred nature of sex and newly-conceived life, the Church acknowledges the critical importance of family in shaping human souls and values.

I learned about parenting the hard way. Not in school, earning degrees, but together with my wife, raising our twelve children and being foster parents to several others.

In fact, much of what I did learn in school I had to unlearn when raising our family. Real life is a great teacher. The tuition is high, but the lessons are powerful. In addition, I have taught a course in parenting skills to more than five hundred parents. I wonder if I taught them as much as they taught me. They helped me to simplify, to get down to basics.

Good parenting is learned. Whether one believes in a

"back to the woodshed" approach or is inclined to give children a little room to grow, a few basic skills emerge. Thanks to my great teachers, my children and all the parents in my classes, I have been able to identify two key principles, on which this book is based. I wish someone had shared these with my wife and me when we started our family.

First, pay attention to behavior you want to encourage. This is called positive reinforcement. Make an organized effort to notice the good behavior when it happens. Give at least as much time to the proper behavior as you do to the undesired behavior.

Second, know that there is much more to discipline than punishment. There has to be. If threats and punishment were a good way to change behavior, TV commercials would be full of threats. After all, advertisers pay a lot of money for their chance at our minds. Yet, there aren't many punitive ads. So why do parents rely so much on threats and punishment? Discipline means learning, not punishing.

That is precisely why McDonald's is a successful business: They get people to do what they want—buy lots of hamburgers, etc.—because they pay attention to the behavior they want. Almost every time you buy something at McDonald's you receive a token reward: free fries, a game coupon, a colored glass, a small Disney character. You are rewarded for the desired behavior; you learn that if you buy food at McDonald's (the "good" behavior), you will be noticed and rewarded (the positive reinforcement). The method works.

My parenting classes taught me another very important lesson. The parents in these classes had all fallen short or failed in some way, but in almost every instance, the failure came when they were severely stressed. As I thought about it, most of my own poor parenting came when I was overly stressed. Hence, any course or book on good parenting ought to deal first with you parents, helping you cope with your life stress. Unless you can handle your own bad moments, it's hard to care wisely and unselfishly for others. McDonald's advertising slogan: "You deserve a break today!" is a good idea. Parents, please take care of yourselves first.

At the same time, parenting needs to be fun. Why not? Children are our windows to wonder, our excuse to play and our tickets to the future.

I thank my children and my students for all they have taught me. I thank them for forcing me to live in the real world, to be practical, to grapple with specific problems and to focus, not on theories, but on results.

CHAPTER ONE

Stress Management

Stress is universal. The person who does not suffer from stress is a person who does not interact and does not accomplish anything. The only way to avoid stress is to avoid action and contact.

Most poor parenting takes place when parents are under stress. Mom and Dad come home from work, tired and discouraged. They are suddenly confronted with the fact that their twelve-year-old son has been caught shoplifting. That's the last straw. Instead of dealing with the news objectively, one parent or both loses their temper and knocks their son down.

Mom is a single parent and has three preschoolers. The weather is hot. The kids are whiny, demanding and pesky. Then four-year-old Laura throws a tantrum to get her way. Instead of ignoring Laura and allowing the tantrum to run its course, Mom goes to her bedroom, slams the door and starts drinking schnapps.

The first step toward learning to be a good parent is learning how to cope with stress. Most of us *do* well when we *feel* well. It's when things are going poorly that we need to be cautious. Learning how to cope with stress means learning to stay in good mental shape most of the time and learning how to act positively and constructively, even when you feel rotten.

Hence you must first take care of yourself. As a parent, you are your child's number one resource. Your energy, your health and your state of mind are major factors in good parenting. It's hard to be a good parent if you are barely hanging on yourself.

While work stress may carry over and affect the home life, most of the examples for stress management in this chapter will concern stress from home life.

The Stress Agents

A stressor or stress agent is a situation that puts pressure on you. As human beings, we face stressors all the time. They come from everywhere.

What are the top stressors for parents? I made the following list of stressors, in rank order, from surveying more than five hundred parents.

1. Money problems

2. Unemployment

3. Marital problems

4. Problems with children

5. Divorce

6. Death of a family member

7. Trouble with friends or neighbors

8. Alcohol or drug problems

Although the parents surveyed have serious problems with their children, notice that they do not list this as their number one problem. Financial, job and marital problems all place more stress on troubled parents and rob them of their precious personal resources so they have that much less energy to deal with child-rearing.

How Stress Feels

Stress is not simply something going on in your head. You may talk of being overwhelmed, of the jitters, of anxiety, of panic. But these feelings are simply the pyschological side of some very real and physical changes taking place in your body.

Suppose I were crossing the street and not watching where I was going. I see a flash of sunlight out of the corner of my eyes and I misinterpret that to be an oncoming car. Here are just a few of the significant changes that will take place in my body, in less than one second, as my emergency nervous system takes command.

1) My pupils will dilate to let in more light so I have large, spook-house eyes.

2) My skin will turn white, because all my outer blood vessels will constrict.

3) I will break out in a cold sweat as my cells discharge waste material and provide a cooling process at the same time.

4) My breathing pattern will change, leaving me to catch my breath.

5) Digestive juices, including potent acids, will be released into my stomach for action. This is why people under prolonged stress are prone to ulcers.

6) My inner blood vessels will expand to automatically handle the increased blood pressure and blood flow.

7) My blood pressure will go up.

8) My heart will beat faster.

9) Coagulants will be secreted into my blood to prevent prolonged bleeding in case of injury.

10) Adrenalin will drop into my blood to enhance my energy and quickness.

11) Neurohormones will be dropped into place between my nerve endings to speed up my senses and to quicken my reaction time.

There is a good reason for these reactions. They ready the body to deal with a crisis. Problems arise, however, when these reactions become a constant state. If something is not done to lessen or relieve the symptoms of stress, they will exact a high toll in both physical breakdown and poorer performance. That is why good parents must first look to themselves, to make sure that they are coping as well as they can with life's many problems.

The Price of Being Tense

This list of physical symptoms helps explain another stress factor which confuses many people. Waiting around can be more exhausting than doing something. The state of readiness described above takes a lot of energy. A spring expends more energy wound up in a state of tension than it does when it goes "sprong" in sudden release.

I once watched a high school doubleheader, two baseball games. In the first game, our pitcher pitched a perfect game, striking out almost everyone. By the end of the game, the shortstop was exhausted. Although he had no chances afield, the effort to stay poised and prepared consumed a lot of energy. Yet to outward appearances, he had done nothing.

In the second game, which we lost 18-13, our shortstop was running all over the diamond. I counted forty-one times that he handled the ball in game play. At the finish, he was exhilarated and wished he might keep on playing.

Nervous inaction can be more demanding and wearing than putting all that available energy to work. That explains why some parents get into the rut of doing less and less, feeling more and more worn out and becoming abrupt and neglectful with their children. Despite the fact that they appear lazy to others, they have no resources left with which to parent. They need to learn to cope first with their own problems; then they can be free to parent with enthusiasm, just as the shortstop in the second game.

Where to Begin Coping

The physical side of stress also gives a clue about some places to begin treating stress. If stress has a physical expression, then it may call for a physical response. Psychological techniques, such as relaxation training and hypnosis, may not be enough. In fact, there are four major ways to treat stress. I think of it as a two-story house, with a basement and a small place next door.

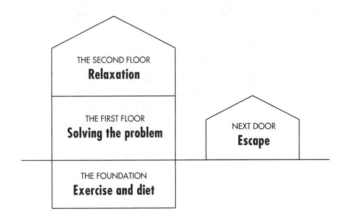

THE SECOND FLOOR
Relaxation

THE FIRST FLOOR
Solving the problem

NEXT DOOR
Escape

THE FOUNDATION
Exercise and diet

The Foundation: Exercise and Diet

Successful stress management begins in the foundation. Be careful about your diet, exercise and sleep. These are the first steps toward taking care of a day or life that may be temporarily out of control. "A sound mind in a sound body"

(*Mens sana in corpore sano*) is more than an obscure Latin inscription found in many school gymnasiums. It is a wise insight that understands the importance of balancing mental health with physical well-being.

Eating Well

"You are what you eat." In times of calm we may get careless about what we eat. Some foods may increase tension. When we find ourselves snappish and short-tempered, exhausted but unable to sleep, then we must pay attention to our edibles.

My first rule: Eat breakfast. Starting a day without breakfast is like running a car engine without oil. After a short time, you will need a valve job, a complete engine overhaul. Coping with the day's troubles without the energy that comes from nourishment can leave you stretched thin with no back-up resources.

Yet so many stressed people skip the day's first meal. Either they are in too much of a hurry, or the oversecretions of their digestive juices make their stomach too jumpy. So they eat nothing at the start of their day, but around ten o'clock, they grab a soft drink and a candy bar for quick energy. That kind of refined sugar diet ensures stress.

Breakfast does not have to be the traditional eggs and toast. For someone in a big hurry, a slice of cheese, or peanut butter or liver sausage spread on whole wheat toast would help a lot. Other quick breakfasts include fresh fruit or juice, whole grain cereals, whole wheat bread or toast, cheese and eggs. Even last night's leftovers can make a tasty breakfast.

Other nutritious foods which may benefit you include fresh fruits and vegetables, lean meats with no preservatives, salads, mixed peanuts and raisins, yogurt and unbuttered, unsalted popcorn. Multiple vitamins fortified with extra B-complex (the stress formula) may help also.

Certain foods are best avoided while you are going through a stressful period. Caffeine and refined sugar are on the no-no list: Caffeine is an energizing drug; refined sugar provides a quick energy fix, making your blood sugar skyrocket and then plummet, causing crankiness, dizziness, weakness and so on. On the other hand, protein and complex carbohydrates raise your blood sugar slowly and keep it steady, providing you the consistent, regular energy source you require to perform well.

Exercising Well

I collapsed when I was forty while playing basketball with my children. After nine days in the hospital, I was told to stop being a weekend athlete. I was in adequate shape for a forty-year-old man, but not for strenuous activities once in a while.

I have always been a Type-A personality. All my life I have had what cardiologists call a labile vascular system. My blood pressure was around 150/90. My regular pulse was in the nineties. And periodically I had some extra and irregular heartbeats.

My children, runners themselves, bought me shorts and shoes, and encouraged me to start jogging. I found it very difficult at first. In fact, it was almost two months before I could trot a mile without some walking.

But once I got in the groove of wogging (walk-jogging) one-and-a-half to two miles at least five times a week, my physiology started to change. After three weeks of steady wogging, my blood pressure dropped to 130/70. My pulse is now in the low sixties. And I have no more extra heartbeats or palpitations. I'm still wogging away.

My experience is common. Research shows that regular exercise releases tranquilizing hormones that reduce your pulse, lower your blood pressure and regularize your breathing, all physical signs of stress when elevated. Hence, regular aerobic exercise reduces stress.

Aerobic exercise stretches the heart and lungs. In this,

it differs from musculoskeletal exercises (e.g., sit-ups, touching your toes and so on), which are designed to develop muscle tone and a trim body.

Examples of aerobic exercise are walking, wogging, running, swimming, walking up and down stairs and bicycling. Other examples include skipping rope, roller skating, rowing, skiing, cross-country skiing and aerobic dancing. Golfing without a cart, handball, basketball and volleyball may be aerobic exercises. A simple indoor method to obtain the aerobic benefit would be stepping on and off a small one-step stool.

How do you know if you are exercising enough to stretch your heart and lungs? A change in breathing pattern and an increase in pulse are the obvious measures. Taking your pulse, however, can be a nuisance. It is much easier to notice the change to a more rapid breathing pattern. Sustaining this heavy breathing without overdoing it and getting out of breath is the key.

How often must you exercise? Once a day for twenty to thirty minutes is the ideal. To get the benefit of healthy physiological changes you need a minimum of fifteen minutes of heavy breathing for a continuous period. This routine must be done at least five times a week.

How to Get to Sleep

Stress can interfere with sleep. Lack of sleep makes the stress symptoms worse. If you go two to three nights without sleep, you can suffer from nervous exhaustion, an overtired and overstimulated state where you lie in bed tossing and turning desperately desiring sleep. Working too hard without adequate leisure time can also induce nervous exhaustion.

You need to learn to relax and rest before you reach the state of nervous exhaustion. Here are some natural and effective ways to encourage relaxation and sleep.

1) Sip a warm drink (milk or decaffeinated tea) about one hour before bedtime.

2) Take a fifteen-minute walk about one hour before bedtime.

3) Take a warm bath (not a shower) about one-half hour before bedtime.

4) Play your favorite tapes as you lie in bed.

5) Read in bed. Read something very different from your daily experience. Good choices could be adventure stories, science fiction or *National Geographic* magazine.

6) Image for relaxation. Picture a favorite scene from your past when you were relaxed and happy. Examine it with your five senses. Recall what it looked like, sounded like, smelled like, felt like, tasted like. This imaging is more interesting and fun than counting sheep.

7) Learn relaxation techniques. Pay attention to your breathing. Count your breaths. Imagine you are exhaling all your tension and worries, and inhaling peace and love. Feel the heavy tension draining out of your limbs and into the bed.

8) Pray. Repeat a prayer over and over. The "Our Father" or one of the psalms are possible choices. Let your mind drift in contemplation of God's marvelous creation. Listen for God's comfort.

9) A good snuggle with or without sexual intimacy with your spouse can help. Loving sexual release can give that impetus to let go of all tension.

10) Engage in some productive activity. If you still can't sleep, get up and do something useful. For one-half hour, clean the house, organize your photo album or write letters. When your eyelids start to close, try again.

Drugs for Stress

Drugs can be helpful in reducing anxiety and stress, but they should be a last resort. Because of the unpredictable side effects of drugs, it is wiser to use natural approaches such as diet and exercise first. However, drugs may be necessary, such as during crisis periods when we need to calm down quickly so we can cope better.

Drugs, however, are only a temporary solution. While drugs may be helpful through a crisis, they are not the best way to reduce stress. When using tranquilizers, allow six weeks for them to take maximum effect. You should begin thinking of reducing and eliminating them after twelve weeks.

Why am I so cautious about drugs? Many of us have become too easy and careless with medicine. Drugs, like surgery, are a radical treatment. Surgery alters the body physically. Drugs change the body chemically. We should use them only when we have exhausted all natural methods, or when the condition is so urgent we do not have time for problem-solving or relaxation techniques. A good example of such a crisis is a racing mind, when your thoughts and worries won't stop. This leads to nervous exhaustion, often accompanied by nausea, upset stomach and lack of appetite.

The first focus for a solution should be on the sleep. If you have gone several nights without sleep, you are probably exhausted. Little else will work until you get some rest. Try the ideas already suggested for getting to sleep. But, if you need sleep tonight, a sleeping pill may be your best *temporary* answer.

The most commonly used "sleepers" today are Dalmane, Ativan, Restoril, Placidyl, Doriden, Phenobarbital and Seconal. All of these require a prescription.

If you are prone to nervous fatigue, you might ask your physician to prescribe up to seven sleeping pills to keep for the times when you have missed at least two nights' sleep and can't afford a third. Take one pill when you first go to bed, not at three o'clock in the morning.

In all of our lives, there are times when the daytime stress is especially severe. If you have tried the other methods to relax and still need some help to take the edge off your anxiety, you may wish to consider a minor tranquilizer. The most commonly used minor tranquilizers are Ativan, Centrax, Librium, Serax, Tranxene, Valium, Xanax, Atarax, Equanil and Miltown.

Medication for sleep or to calm shattered nerves can be a godsend in a crisis situation to get you back on track. Don't use drugs, however, as a first resort or as the usual way to calm your nerves. Keep them for emergencies only.

The First Floor: Solving the Problem

Learning ways to solve hard problems is a skill every parent needs. The first step in problem solving is to know your resources and be able to use them as needed.

Know Your Resources

You are not alone. When you become overwhelmed, it is easy to get locked in on a particular problem and fail to see all the possible resources that might help. You need to take inventory of your inner strengths, family and friends who might be available to help and, if possible, resources within the community. Here is a list of some of the places you might look. These are but some of the resources that can be used to remedy and reduce the very real problems that cause stress, problems like poverty, unemployment, the need for child care, loneliness and alcoholism.

Three Resource Levels

Inner personal
Family and friends
Community

1) Energy. Without it, you are lost. Follow the suggestions discussed earlier to eat right and get rest so you'll have the physical energy to cope.

2) Health. If you have any questions or concerns, a physical exam may be a wise idea.

3) Time. You may need to take time-outs for yourself to do something you enjoy, to let your anger subside or to reflect on your problems directly.

4) Positive attitude. Your attitude is the emotional coloring with which you greet the day. You need an "I can do it" approach, not a defeatist one. So lighten up, brighten up, smile and keep telling yourself you can do it.

5) Ideas. Without ideas, you are lost. Trials can dull your mind. Stress puts blinders on you and you're apt to see only one path. To find a way over the problem causing you stress, you need to open up your mind to other options, pathways to solutions, depending on the particular problem. For example, if you have problems with finances, perhaps you need to think of ways other than getting a second job to make money, e.g., collecting aluminum cans, working at home (maybe one of your hobbies can be turned into a money-making venture), holding a garage sale.

6) Job. Unemployment or job dissatisfaction can be debilitating. If you have a job that you like, count your blessings. If you feel bored or underemployed, investigate your options for other opportunities in your field or other careers. Arrange for some free time to spend in the local public library. Enlist the help of a reference librarian to find and use the information sources that might lead to a refreshed or new career for you.

7) Money. Even though you may feel you never have enough, some people lack the minimum to provide

necessities or find themselves overwhelmed by bills and debt. While you cannot afford a professional financial adviser, you can call your local consumer credit counseling service, which offers several free services. They can teach you how to set up a basic budget, intervene on your behalf with your creditors and negotiate favorable payment plans for you that protect your credit rating and counsel you on individual problems unique to your family's situation.

8) Education. There are many ways to learn in addition to formal schooling at a high school, college or technical school. Going to the library, using a computer teaching program, enrolling in community education courses or learning new skills on your job can be effective ways to improve your assets and your self-image.

Family and Friends

1) Talk with a friend. The coffee klatsch may be the oldest and best way to deal with stress. Use the telephone. Friends can provide a listening ear and emotional support. Friends can also be counted on in a crisis to provide tangible help, such as chauffeuring, a loan or a place to stay for a few days.

2) Use your parents and grandparents, if you live close to them. They often make the best babysitters because they care the most and cost the least. If you live too far away from them, enlist the help of your friends. Perhaps start a cooperative arrangement with other parents, exchanging babysitting services instead of money.

3) Talk to your siblings. Maybe you feel you did not get along that well as children, but family can usually be counted on in an emergency.

4) Enlist your children's help. Everyone wants to be needed, especially children. They can help with many chores and household tasks, from cooking meals to washing clothes.

Community Resources

1) Self-help groups. These are groups of people who have been there, the real experts. Examples are Alcoholics Anonymous (AA), Weight Watchers, Tough Love (dealing with rebellious teens), Parents Anonymous and Recovery (dealing with depression). Check the telephone directory for the phone number of the local group or call your library or appropriate social services agency for the address of the particular national organization to put you in touch with the local group. If you don't find a group that matches your particular concern, call a few like-minded neighbors and start one.

2) Recreational activities. Learn what your community has to offer: city and state parks, campgrounds, roller rinks, bowling alleys, movie theaters, swimming pools, museums. You can supplement the community offerings by gathering some favorite entertainments in your own home. VCR video games and movie tapes have become popular; so are music audiocassettes, table games and jigsaw puzzles.

3) Churches. Most churches offer far more than religious services. They usually have active study groups and support groups. Also, the minister is often a good counselor and resource for help.

4) Day care. The best reference for a good day-care center or babysitter will come from parents who have been satisfied with their services. Check with your friends about good child-care facilities.

5) Head Start. Your physically or mentally handicapped preschool child is probably eligible for special early schooling through the Head Start program.

6) Thrift shops and yard sales. Most communities have developed a variety of recycling possibilities whereby used clothes, furniture and appliances are sold at a very low cost.

7) Gardens. An indoor or outdoor garden, for food or decoration, can be a stress-reducing and money-saving hobby.

8) Welfare department. The welfare department is best known for providing money when income is low, particularly through its Aid for Dependent Children (AFDC) and food stamp programs. Also available are homeowners who come in to teach budgeting, cleaning, cooking and other household management skills.

9) Probation office. Rather than view the probation office as the enemy, parents can welcome the support and clout of a good probation officer in controlling unruly teens. At the early signs of trouble, parents might ask the probation officer to endorse the family curfew rules and chore assignments. This is called informal probation. If the child fails to comply, more formal charges can be filed.

10) Youth services bureau. This type of agency goes by a wide variety of names. Most communities have some sort of organization that runs a teen center with recreational facilities, other teen programs, alternative education programs for youngsters suspended from school and teen self-help groups for alcohol and substance abuse, suicide prevention and other difficulties.

11) Social Security. This federal program can provide regular financial assistance to disabled children and adults or to the children of deceased or disabled parents.

12) Medicare and Medicaid. Here are two programs that provide medical insurance: Medicaid for those receiving welfare assistance and Medicare for retired and disabled persons.

13) Food pantry. Most communities, often through churches, have banded together to provide emergency food on request for hungry persons and families.

14) WIC. This acronym is short for Women, Infants and Children. The program provides free food for young mothers and their babies.

15) Public health nurse. Free immunizations are available in the public health office.

16) County extension office. This agency provides information on everything from making drapes to rearing children, from canning food to training puppies, from exterminating roaches to changing the oil in your car. Free pamphlets are available on many subjects.

17) Library. People may have forgotten what a valuable resource the public library can be: as a source of information about job openings and current events through daily papers and magazines, as a source of self-education through books on all types of skills and subjects, as a source of free recreation through novels and videotapes and as a place to enjoy adult programs. For the children, there is often a regular story hour, which can give you some free time.

18) Energy assistance program. Most public utilities offer a special program, e.g., Project Safe, that helps needy families pay their winter energy bills.

19) Job training programs. The Job Training Partnership Act (JTPA) provides job training and employment services for economically disadvantaged youth and adults, dislocated workers and others who face significant employment problems.

20) Transportation. Check with your local bus system and taxi services. Most communities provide transportation for medical and shopping trips.

21) Mental health clinic. A variety of services, including counseling, child guidance, group sessions and educational programs are often available at the mental health center in your community.

22) Service clubs. Rotary, Lions, Kiwanis and other local community service organizations can sometimes be called upon to provide financial help for the handicapped or other special purposes.

23) Rent (subsidized housing). Almost every community has some housing where rents are supplemented by the federal government so that renters with a lack of funds can pay according to their income.

24) Family crisis center. This is a place to go temporarily to escape from spouse abuse. Food and shelter are provided.

One Day at a Time

Stress is best handled one day at a time. Set priorities. Make a list of jobs to tackle and problems that need solving. Then tackle them one day at a time. If you try to solve them all at once you will be like the telephone switchboard operator with forty incoming calls. You will be overwhelmed, start pulling out all the connections in desperation and end up accomplishing nothing.

Do it! Begin with something small and easy. This is called "first-stepping." Any movement in the right direction is progress.

Be very concrete and specific, no vague resolutions such as: "I need a more positive attitude." Instead start with realistic items such as: (a) I will call about the job listed in the paper immediately after lunch. (b) I will clean house from one-thirty to two-thirty this afternoon. (c) I will sit on the front porch and wait for the kids to come home from school to greet them.

Not all problems can be resolved through practical steps. Some problems need to be worked around, and others must be accepted as a part of life. This wisdom is best summarized in the Serenity Prayer written in 1934 by Reinhold Niebuhr:

O God, give us the serenity to accept what cannot be changed, courage to change what should be changed, and wisdom to distinguish the one from the other.

Stressed people need the serenity such an approach can bring.

Problem-Solving Skills

While much of stress is highly emotional, you can approach and attempt to resolve many of the stressors rationally in a logical sequence. Here are nine steps:

1) Make a list of all your problems.

2) Gather information. When you are under stress it is easy to feel boxed in, as if there were only one way out and the door was locked. You need to explore any and every other possible way out, all the resources and people who might help and all the other ways of handling the problems, which for the moment seem hopeless. Talk to your friends and family. Explore all the possible solutions you can.

3) Brainstorm. Review all the information you have gathered, and try to think of any other possibilities, even ones that seem crazy at first. Get yourself in a relaxed mood. Meet with other people. Encourage them to say whatever comes to their minds. Consider everything.

4) Make a list of all the possible solutions to each problem.

5) Consider the advantages and disadvantages of each possible solution. Write them down in two separate columns.

6) Consider your feelings. Some solutions may make sense but may go against your strong feelings. It comes as no surprise that much of our stress is related to our feelings.

7) Choose a solution that best meets your needs and situation.

8) Break down each acceptable solution into manageable and concrete steps so you know exactly what you are going to do and where to get started.

9) Get started. Give it a try. Do something. Begin with an easy first step to get yourself going.

10) Review and reward yourself: R and R. Keep track of what you have done on a calendar, in your journal or on a chart designed for this purpose. Give yourself a small reward or treat for each step forward.

Next Door: Escape—Get Away From It All

Before ascending to the second floor of the problem-solving house and considering some of the mental techniques for dealing with stress, take a break. Go next door and get away for a moment. As an anonymous poet said: "He that fights and runs away may live to fight another day."

Sometimes things are too difficult to face right now. A temporary escape may be necessary. When the basketball team seems to have forgotten everything it had worked on and cannot even get the ball to mid-court, it's time to stop. The coach signals a "T" and the referee blows the whistle for a time-out.

A time-out can also be used as a preventive measure. Smart people schedule breaks and vacations into their days and lives in anticipation of stress. After all, vacations *are* cheaper than hospitals and a lot more fun! Indeed, in Europe, a visit to a health spa is covered by medical insurance.

Take a Break

Everyone should schedule breaks into the day. Large corporations, not always known for compassion toward their employees, often insist that their workers take a fifteen-minute coffee break both in the morning and afternoon. The reason for their insistence: The quantity and quality of employees' work is usually improved.

An example of a parenting situation that almost demands a break is raising a hyperactive child. A hyperactive child can stretch anyone's resources. Like other therapists, I use many techniques in treating hyperactivity. The one element I always insist upon, however, is diversion—for the parent. The parent caring for a hyperactive child needs some time each day to get away and re-collect herself.

Daydreaming is one common diversion. If things become too hard or boring, the mind wanders. Alcohol is another way some choose to take a break. Many people drink to dull their pain or to slow down their racing mind or just to "relax and have a good time." Daydreaming and alcohol at times can provide a good interruption for a stressful period. They can also be dangerous escapes, however, if used as a regular and only program of relaxation.

The best way to take a *healthy* break is to *plan* your breaks. Perhaps plan to watch your favorite TV show in mid-morning or mid-afternoon: It's something for you to look forward to. Or you may need to find a way to get out of the house for a little while. A leisurely bath may provide a welcome and self-indulgent interlude. Bathrooms with locks can even be good places to hide for a moment or two.

Plan daily and weekly breaks. They don't have to cost money. Use your imagination to schedule a night out. Don't hesitate to get a babysitter to give yourself relief. If you cannot afford one, find other parents with whom you can trade babysitting services.

And Now for Something Entirely Different

The Kenny thirteen-week plan is a way of planning a break each week and learning new ways to recreate at the same time. Scheduling is necessary. If you wait for the mood to strike and motivate you, you are not likely to try something different when you need it most. Moreover, you are not at your most creative and energetic when you feel tired, tense and overwhelmed.

Here's how to get the Kenny thirteen-week plan into operation.

1) Get yourself one of those large kitchen calendars, with an empty square around each date.

2) Convene a family meeting.

3) Take turns selecting something to do each week.

4) Be specific. Select a date, time and place. Depending on the activity, you may select an evening, a morning or a weekend afternoon. Write it on your calendar.

5) The same activity cannot be selected twice. You must do thirteen different things.

6) Be imaginative. Here is a sample list you and your family might choose.

> Week one. Thursday, 7 p.m.: Dad and Mom go out to dinner.
>
> Week two. Thursday, 7 p.m.: The entire family goes into the bathroom, fills the tub, turns out the light and bobs for apples. One apple has a quarter in it.
>
> Week three. Sunday, 1 p.m.: Shop at the mall.
>
> Week four. Thursday, 7 p.m.: Family members take turns standing on their heads and singing the high school song.
>
> Week five. Saturday, noon: Cook lunch in the backyard.
>
> Week six. Thursday, 7 p.m.: The entire family goes to the roller rink.

Week seven. Saturday, 9 a.m.: The entire family goes bowling.

Week eight. Sunday, 5 a.m.: The entire family gets up to watch the sun rise. Then they have breakfast together.

Week nine. Thursday, 7 p.m.: The family plays Monopoly®.

Week ten. Saturday, 6 p.m. to 12 a.m.: The family rents three John Wayne movies and has a film festival with popcorn and punch.

Week eleven. Sunday, 1 p.m.: Everyone goes shopping together and buys three ingredients for a crazy salad bar buffet. Anything goes, even M&M's®.

Week twelve. Thursday, 7 p.m.: Look through the family photo albums.

Week thirteen. Sunday, 1 p.m.: The family goes for a hike in a nearby state or county park.

Mini Breaks

A very good way to break the cycle of tension is to interrupt, however briefly, what you are doing. Don't tell yourself to relax. That won't work. Instead, *do* something different for a moment. Here are some suggestions for ways to turn off your daily stress for a brief period so that you may resume your tasks refreshed.

Sleep late.

Polish your shoes.

Say a prayer.

Read a label.

Wash your hair.

Walk instead of ride.

Take a bubble bath.

Rent a video.

Compliment yourself.

Make faces in the mirror.

Contact a long-neglected friend.

Slow down.

Answer a question.

Paint your face with body paint.

Gaze at the stars.

Visit a shut-in person.

Cry a little.

Start a tradition.

Ask for help.

Jump for joy.

Make your own candles.

Sing a song.

Invite company over.

Send for travel folders.

Laugh with your family.

Run around the house twice.

Listen to classical music.

Honk your horn.

Read a poem aloud.

Make up a "clean" swear word.

Drink a glass of orange juice.

Yell at the top of your lungs.

Emphasize your best qualities.

Be a gracious receiver.

Put seed in the bird feeder.

Smile.

Develop Outside Activities

In addition to breaks, it helps to cultivate favorite activities to fall back on in times of stress, such as a hobby, a skill, something you like to do.

For some people, this activity may be a walk or a run. Or it may be pulling out the photo album to insert the latest batch of pictures, baking bread, working on the car, going fishing or puttering around the garage workshop.

Some parents get so locked into their jobs and parenting duties that they forget their hobbies and pastimes. Ask them what they like to do and they draw a blank. This is a problem.

If you don't have a hobby or skill, develop one. This may be the time to learn a new art or craft, despite the fact that you feel over-stressed. Some hobbies are quilting, rug making, crocheting, metal work, ceramics, guitar playing, sewing, learning to use a synthesizer, woodworking, growing plants, gardening and piano playing. In stressful times, it's wise to get your hands and feet busy with something *away* from the stress.

Use Your Friends

The most common and important remedy for stress is to contact a friend. Two-thirds of persons facing difficult moments get in touch with a friend. Friends are chosen before family members, probably because family members often are the source of some of the stress.

Don't be shy. Use your friends. That's what friendship is for. A friend can be a sounding board, helping you get things off your chest and out in the open where you may be able to see the situation a little more clearly. Friends can also provide additional ideas when you get locked in a rut and can see only one way out. Friends can provide tangible help, anything from a borrowed cup of sugar to an evening of babysitting. Friends can provide emotional support. Smiles, hugs and other strokes of encouragement keep us going.

So pick up the phone. Put on the coffee pot. Or get in the car and go seek out your friends. Use them and they will feel free to call on you when they feel that life is asking too much of them.

The Second Floor: Relaxation

Finally, it is time to climb to the second floor of the house and consider psychological remedies for stress. Although stress is clearly not all in your mind, your mind can be a powerful tool for solving problems and restoring your body to its normal physical way of functioning.

Hopefully, you have already built your foundation on proper diet, exercise and rest. You have taken practical steps to resolve your problems as best you can. And you have planned loopholes or breaks into your daily life. Now for the finishing touch: Learn some ways your mind can bring your body under control. Probably your friends have already told you at nervous moments to calm down or relax. That advice usually doesn't work because it doesn't tell you *how* to relax. In fact, that "command" often makes you more tense. Here are some techniques that could work better for you.

Learn to Laugh

A sense of humor appears to be uniquely human. Animals don't laugh. Yet humans smile and laugh at wonderfully inappropriate times, when life seems to have suddenly become very heavy.

Laughter, like rage, is an explosive emotion. It is a marvelous way to reduce the tension of bound-up anxiety or to break the lethargic cycle of "I don't care" hopelessness that accompanies depression. Laughter can't be forced, but when it happens, it is like the sun breaking through dark clouds for a moment.

Humor is the sudden grasping of a paradox, the insight that things aren't supposed to be this way: a man acting like a monkey or things getting so bad that nothing worse could possibly happen—and then it does. That can seem funny.

Have you ever had one of those days when everything went wrong, until things got so awful that you simply began to laugh, albeit a bit hysterically? I remember the day our daughter, Bitta, was born. My wife, Mary, had been in labor for two days, and I had been up all night. Bitta was born at eight in the morning and I felt weary but very good.

Around noon, as a clinical psychologist at the college, I was suddenly faced with a crisis. A student in the dorm had a knife and was trying to decide whether to kill himself or his roommate. While talking on three phones and trying to coordinate a sane and safe response with the police, the college staff and other students, a fourth phone rang. The elementary school was calling to tell me that a swing had broken off my son Mike's two new adult front teeth and he was in great pain. Of course, it was the dentist's day off. After an hour I finally located Dr. Miller on the golf course, and he agreed to pick up Mike at school.

We resolved the student crisis without tragedy. I went home feeling a bit battered, but mildly pleased that I had handled a few disasters without caving in. Dr. Miller met me at the door. The bad news was that the root canals cost two-hundred and fifty dollars each. Oh well.

Mike and I went into the house and on to the kitchen, where Barbara, our babysitter, was watching our four small children and three of her own. As I walked into the kitchen, our electric stove blew up. No reason; it just picked that very moment to go off like a Roman candle. Bits of melted burner flew all around the kitchen, starting two secondary fires. I just stood there numb. Barbara shoved the stove aside and pulled the plug.

Fortunately, none of the children were burned. That was the good news. The bad news was that the stove was a total and hopeless mess, melted down like the Wicked Witch of the West at the end of *The Wizard of Oz*.

On my way to the hospital that night to visit my wife and new daughter, planning on how I was going to tell her of the day's events, I smiled. Then I started to chuckle. Then came peals of laughter. I could hardly wait until she asked me: "And how was *your* day?"

Learn to Reward Yourself

Life can be very difficult and sometimes the steps we have to take to face our troubles or get ourselves up and moving out of a depressive rut can seem impossible. Learn to give yourself mini-rewards for each small step you take in the right direction.

The reward can be very simple, such as merely keeping track of what you have done. Check off each item on your *To Do* list as you accomplish it. Write down the number of miles you have bicycled or minutes you have exercised on your calendar. Count the number of rooms you have cleaned or the loads of laundry washed, dried and put away. Give yourself credit.

Give GTMs (Good to Myselfs). Follow a difficult time with your favorite music or a special treat. If you are a homemaker, clean house from nine to ten in the morning and then sit down to read your favorite book or watch your favorite television show. Work with your son on his homework from eight-thirty to nine and then raid the refrigerator together to make a special salad with six "you-pick-em" items.

Learn to Say No

Remember the best-selling book *Don't Say Yes When You Mean to Say No*[1]? Good advice. Parents who care can find themselves overextended.

"Yes, I'll help my daughter with her homework each night...."

"Of course, I'll bake cookies for the class party...."

"If no one else can be Brownie den mother, I'll give it a try...."

"Sure, I'll chauffeur the girls home from their practice after school...."

"You say you volunteered me to be Band Booster secretary? Well, OK...."

It is too easy to take on too many tasks. Both addition and subtraction are learned early in our education, but some of us were never very good at subtracting. We just kept adding things.

Learn to say no. That's the first step. Practice it. Imagine yourself saying it on the phone next time you are asked to assume another responsibility. You don't have to give your reasons or explain yourself. Just say no.

The second step involves prioritizing your current activities. List them all; then try rating each activity from one to five. Give a one to activities you have to do or you enjoy so much you would miss them terribly if you stopped. Rate the other activities by their importance to you, with five being the least important. This is a sensible way to order your priorities.

Keep the "ones" and draw your cutoff line somewhere down the list. Call or write the parties involved with those activities that fall below the cutoff line and tell them: "I'm sorry to resign. I have to cut back in order to take care of

[1] Fenstrheim, Herb. New York, New York: McKay, 1975.

my family and me first. I have enjoyed working with you."

Pray

Prayer is not often mentioned as a stress reduction technique. Or if it is, it's the prayer of petition, the kind of prayer that goes: "God, help me to get well" or "God, send more money." Eventually, if the prayer appears to go unanswered, the person becomes discouraged and stops.

There are two other types of prayer that may be more helpful. The first is to find a prayer that expresses your feelings. The Book of Psalms is one good source. "Out of the depths I have cried to you, O Lord...." Here are a lot of poems by hurting people not so much asking for relief as describing how they feel.

Look through the psalms and copy down part of one that fits how you feel. Change the words to describe better your own state. Write it on an index card and carry it in your purse or wallet. Pull it out and repeat it over and over in bad moments during the week.

Similarly, the words from most country-western music describe the pain of broken hearts, rejection, job loss and depression. Sing a sad song and get in touch with the pain of other hurting people. Offer your song to God as a description of how you feel.

The response from the Litany Against Fear, repeated by the Bene Gesserit order, in the best-selling science fiction thriller *Dune*, is still another example: "I must not fear. Fear is the mind-killer. Fear is the little-death that brings total obliteration. I will face my fear. I will permit it to pass over me and through me. And when it has gone past I will turn the inner eye to see its path. Where the fear has gone there will be nothing. Only I will remain."[2]

The second type of prayer is more like meditation. Fix in your mind a religious scene and focus gently on it. A Catholic saying the rosary, repeating Hail Marys while

[2] Herbert, Frank. *Dune*. New York, New York: Ace Books, 1987, p. 8.

meditating on mysteries like the annunciation and incarnation, is one good example.

Meditate on God's concern for the lilies of the field and for each and every sparrow. Let his peace and love fill your soul more and more with every breath you take.

Or select a mantra for each day to fit your needs. A mantra is a special word, theme or slogan to help you stay focused in the right direction. Examples of prayerful mantras are "Peace," "Love," "Everything in God's Hands," "May the Spirit be with you!," "Praise the Lord" and so on.

Learn Ways to Relax

Of the many specific programs for mental relaxation, tension/relaxation, imaging and breathing are the most popular.

Tension/Relaxation (TR). Relaxation is achieved by first exaggerating the muscle tension for about ten seconds and then letting go of that physical tension.

Progress through each major muscle group in your body one by one, slowly.

> Tense your [name of muscle, e.g., calf] muscle.
>
> Hold it tight.
>
> Feel the heavy tension: wired, wound up, tight, in pain.
>
> You feel like you can't continue to hold it....
>
> And now let it go.
>
> Ahhh!

Feel the good feeling that comes and spreads when the muscle, like a rubber band, returns to its normal length and the blood starts flowing through it again.

Follow the same process for each of your muscle groups:

Your forehead. (Raise your eyebrows.)

Your jaws. (Bite down.)

Your neck. (Scrunch your head down.)

Your upper back. (Pull your shoulders together behind your back.)

Your biceps. (Make a muscle.)

Your hands. (Make a fist.)

Your abdomen. (Pull in your tummy.)

Your calves. (Point your toes toward you.)

Imaging. Imaging is simple to learn. Recall a scene from your own past that was pleasant and free from stress. Then use all five senses to examine it. What does it look like? What do you hear? What do you smell? How does it taste? How does it feel?

Telling yourself to relax usually is ineffective. But picturing a relaxing scene and continuing to draw your mind gently back to the details of that scene work much better. Here is a sample of how imaging might be used:

Imagine you are settling down on a warm beach.

You are alone.

Feel the sand fit itself to your body as you snuggle in.

You can feel the warm sun caressing your body like a mother's touch.

Remember how, when you were a child, you used to look up and wonder:

How high is the sky?

What makes it so blue?

And you watched the tumbling clouds drifting by, changing shapes, and you played guessing games:

35

Now it looks like a dog and now an Indian head.

Notice those two seagulls floating and drifting back and forth.

So lazy,
catching an air current up,
gliding down,
so high.

You can hear them calling to one another,

"Caw! Caw!"

Smell the ocean breeze:
that unmistakable mixture of seaweed and brine and fish,
so outdoorsy and healthy.

And taste it.

If you lick your lips you can taste the salt.

But most of all, listen.

Listen to the rhythm of the incoming waves
washing up against the shore
one after another after another
as they have done for centuries and centuries before
you and I were born,
and will do for centuries and centuries after you and I
are gone,
washing up with a rhythm that is nature's own
heartbeat.

Let your heart beat in rhythm with the incoming
waves.

Let your breathing be in pattern with the gentle
breezes.

Reflect.

You are part of the celebration of existence.

You are never truly alone.

You are a cousin to the sand and the water,
a sister to the fish and birds and all living things.

You are a daughter of the sun.

You are a child of the universe.

And you have a right to be.

Breathing. Finally, there are many relaxation techniques
that call for you to focus on your breathing. This is a nice
method to practice, since if you are good at it, relaxation
can be but a breath away. Here is a sample.

Pay attention to your breathing.

Let all other distractions dance around the outside of
your mind
like so many shadows in a candle-lit room
and keep bringing your mind's eye back to your
breathing.

Take a deep breath.

Hold it! Hold it!

And now let it go.

And feel the good feeling that comes and spreads
when you let go of tension.

Breathing in——oxygen,

Breathing out——carbon dioxide.

Breathing in——health,

Breathing out——all your aches and pains.

Breathing in——peace,

Breathing out——all your tensions and worries.

When I was a small child

I read the question in the catechism.

"Where is God?"

And the very beautiful answer:

"God is everywhere. He is in the very air you breathe."

So you are also breathing in God's own loving concern for you.

Imagine you can follow each breath as it enters your lungs.

And begins to spread throughout your bloodstream and your entire body.

You can feel the oxygen going into your lungs
and entering the alveoli,
those tiny pockets in the corners of your lungs
where the oxygen is transferred to your capillaries
and carried by these tiny blood vessels to your
arteries.

You can feel the oxygen-rich blood spreading
up your neck and into your head,
a very light and warm feeling,
as if your head were a hard sponge
and this were soft warm water,
gentling and soothing,
smoothing out the wrinkles in your forehead,
washing over your jaw muscles.

You are becoming more and more relaxed
with each breath.

The good feeling is spreading into your upper back
like the massage of a thousand tiny fingers,
dancing across your upper back
untying each knotted muscle.

The good feeling is spreading into your arms
down to your fingertips.

You are becoming calmer and calmer

with each breath.

The good feeling is spreading to your tummy
and lower back
and hips
as if you were seated in a warm water bath.

Imagine it as a Jacuzzi
with the warm water bubbling and splashing
around you
washing away all the heavy tension.

See it dissolve in the water like dirt
carried away down the drain
becoming more and more at peace with each breath.

The good feeling is spreading into your thighs
and the calves of your legs.

Imagine rubbing and massaging your legs,
feeling so good.

The good feeling is spreading down
to your feet and toes.

You are continuing to relax and feel peace
more and more with each breath.

Parents, like everyone else, feel stress. Unless you first take care of yourself and cope with your stress, you will find it very difficult to be a good parent.

Start with the obvious physical remedies, such as exercise, diet and sleep. Identify and work on your problems in a systematic and rational way. Take breaks regularly and when you need them. And learn to relax.

So much for your personal needs. Let's talk now about parenting.

CHAPTER TWO

The Good Enough Parent

Good enough (GE) parenting consists of the three L's: living, loving and learning. The GE parent provides a living: room and board. Often such a parent works hard at a second job to provide a little extra, to save for college, and in return often feels taken for granted, with little gratitude.

That, however, does not deter the GE parent, who continues to be loving. This type of parental love knows no conditions, asks for nothing in return. Like God's love for us, a parent's love keeps right on, whatever happens.

Learning is the third element of GE parenting. Learning is the true meaning of the word "discipline." Primarily, this book is about the third parental task: teaching and learning.

With smaller families, many parents feel extra pressure to raise their children very well. With both parents working, or with divorce, parents put considerable emphasis on "quality time," making the most of their minimal time available and still doing a first-rate job.

There is danger in these scenarios. Parents will aspire to be perfect. When, because their child has some problems, they think they are failing, parents' reaction is predictable. First, they will overdose the child with love, trying to buy good behavior through good parent-child communication and gratitude. When that doesn't work, they may get frustrated and revert to a "woodshed" approach (i.e., "take the child to the woodshed for a 'good' strapping"), upping the penalty (the strapping) when that method still doesn't achieve compliance.

What happens when the inexperienced parent comes head to head with the rebel years in child-rearing: the terrible twos and the unlucky (for parents) thirteens? Parents may naively assume they are doing something wrong during these years. When the parents cannot figure out what they are doing wrong, the next step often is to blame their child for not being a better person.

A lot of the pressure would ease up if parents did not burden themselves with such high and unrealistic expectations. To be a perfect parent, you need perfect children. As one wag put it: "I'd have been a wonderful parent, if it weren't for my children." To be perfect, you must understand your standards. Do you want well-behaved children, babies who sleep through the night, children who go to church, children who are free to speak their minds, children who achieve good grades, children who are strong enough to buck the system?

The problem with any of these standards is that children never hold still. No matter what you have now, they keep changing. Child-rearing, like life itself, is a process, not a product. So relax. You're in it for the long haul, through good times and bad. Never give up. And hang on to the idea that you are a good enough parent.

Making a Living

Many hardworking parents spend their whole lives providing for their children. They do so at great sacrifice. They come home at night with few if any physical or emotional reserves. They are not at their best. Then, if something goes wrong, perhaps the child "smarts off," the parent loses his or her temper and beats the child. That behavior may not be acceptable but it can be understood. The parent was tired and acted out of that fatigue. In fact, the effort to be a good provider is what led up to the exhaustion and the child abuse.

I saw many good parents in my class who were referred

for child abuse. They gave their children everything. They loved and cared. And in a stressful moment, they lost their cool and good sense.

If you are a hardworking parent, don't take out your fatigue and stress on your child. Find some other way of relief. But at the same time, remember *why* you are working so hard. You care. Food and shelter are the essence of taking care of someone. You are providing bed and board, keeping body and soul together. You *are* a GE parent.

Loving

Loving means all your listening, hugs and shared tears. Loving means reaching back for untested resources, giving when you have nothing left to give, stretching your heart farther and wider than you thought possible.

There are two kinds of love: conditional and unconditional. Conditional love is better known as discipline. That is the love we provide when our children behave themselves or achieve. "I love you if you do your jobs; if you don't fight with your brother; if you earn good grades." Conditional love teaches us which way to go and to be responsive to the needs and wishes of other people.

But all of us, especially children, need to be affirmed with unconditional love, the love that continues no matter what we do, the love with no strings attached. "I love you just because you're you." What person, young or old, is not lifted and warmed by such a message?

Infants need and flourish on unconditional love alone. Parents don't make demands on infants. The understanding parent loves the baby whether or not the baby sleeps through the night. And whether or not the infant cries or spits up is irrelevant. Nothing the baby does causes the parents to withdraw love.

All babies need unconditional love. Understanding, loving parents feel, "It is all right for you to wake up during the night, little one. Schedules were made by and for adults, not infants. It is all right for you to cry just to be held. Holding is just as important to you as food."

As the baby grows, parents introduce conditional love. "I love you if you stay dry at night, if you do your homework, if you make the varsity team, if you go to college." The child, however, whether three years old or sixteen years old, still needs unconditional love, and the place to find it is in the home. School, jobs and competitive sports all offer conditional love. In these activities, you must perform to be loved. But home remains the one place people welcome you, care about you and love you just because you are you.

Some things all of us have in common: None of us is perfect; every one of us thirsts for love; we all need to be loved for our own sake regardless of our talents or lack thereof. In homes where people love one another unconditionally, the strengths and weaknesses of all the members are graciously accepted. We all need a loving base, whether we deserve it or not.

Such unconditional love is the foundation of GE parenting. Read more about it as a preventive discipline in Chapter Four. From the onset of toddlerhood, parents need to set and enforce an increasing number of expectations so the children can learn to survive in a rough world. But underneath it all, there needs to be an abiding message: "I love you, whatever you do or say. My love is always there, forgiving and warm."

Discipline Means Learning

The origin of the word "discipline" means "teaching" or "learning." Punishment is one way to discipline, though not a very effective way, and certainly not the only way to teach or encourage learning. Unfortunately, the word "discipline" has become equated with punishment.

Jesus had many disciples. They were people who followed him, who learned from him. They were not people he regularly punished. He was firm, yet very compassionate. And his way of handling people changed lives.

Everyone would like to change the behavior of someone else. Parents especially would like to change their children's behavior. A positive approach, with attention paid to the good behavior, works better.

The LYP Method

Yet too many parents use the LYP method of discipline: Lecture-Yell-Punish. When making a request or attempting to stop misbehavior, parents begin by explaining. When the child does not jump to obey, the parents add more reasons, all of them quite sensible. Parents tend to keep on lecturing because it sounds so good. They are making the right demands for the right reasons. But does it work? Not too often and not too well.

When parents run out of reasons, they raise their voices, louder and louder. The child is not listening. The parents believe a loud firm voice ought to compel the child to pay attention and obey. Does that work? Again, not as often as parents would wish.

When a raised voice fails, parents revert to threats or punishment, such as a denial of privileges: "No TV tonight." "You're grounded." Perhaps a spanking is administered. How sad because there is another and better way to obtain good behavior from children.

The first thing to remember is that bad behavior is learned. If it is learned, it can also be unlearned. And good behavior can be taught in its place, but not by long lectures.

Good discipline is neither automatic nor magical. Rather, it is a very real skill that parents can learn. The steps are simple enough. Here they are.

Positive Parenting

1) *Target* your goals carefully and selectively. Any behavior that can be observed is a potential target for parental discipline. The wisdom comes in knowing which of the many child behaviors to select for attention. First preference should always be given to rewarding desirable behavior, simply because it is much more economical to focus your parental time and attention on good behavior than on misbehavior.

2) *Be positive.* Find a way of rewarding successes rather than punishing failures or misbehavior. Time and attention are rewarding, even if they are negative. Why waste time and attention on bad behavior? As most parents know well, lecturing rarely stops the bad behavior, even though the lecture may sound great. The better approach is to identify a bad behavior such as fighting, too much noise or coming home late; then figure out the opposite behavior such as playing cooperatively and quietly or coming home on time, and reward the good behavior.

3) *Start small.* Begin where the child is, not where you want the child to be. Begin with what is already happening, and reward any movement in the right direction. Break larger tasks into smaller units, and reward each small success. A good example might be cleaning up a messy room. Instead of simply demanding that a child clean up the room, divide the job into units—"make your bed," "pick up your toys from the floor," "put the dirty clothes in the hamper," "clean off the dresser top" and so on. Give credit for each small accomplishment.

4) *Be concrete and specific.* Select behaviors that can be observed and counted. Much discipline fails to work because the target is too vague. Goals such as a good attitude, respect and a sense of responsibility are too general. Ask yourself what the child needs to do to show a "good attitude." Then reward that good attitude

when it happens.

5) *Be consistent.* Consistency does not mean that you cannot change your disciplinary goals. It does mean that you must stick to your word, and, if and when you change your plan, you must keep your child aware of what you expect and why. And, in two-parent families or with shared parenting arrangements, parents need to agree with each other, and to follow through on their word with the children, day after day.

6) *Keep score with charts.* Charting is a good way to get a new discipline plan started. Basketball coaches keep track of points, rebounds and assists. Factory supervisors keep track of production. They call it statistics. Parents do well when they keep statistics on the good behavior of their children.

Charting behavior is a fun way to keep track of the behavior you want; call it behavioral bookkeeping. The chart is a written record of the date and target behavior with space for smile-faces, stars or stickers to reward the desired behavior when it occurs. Charting works.

CHAPTER THREE

Anything for Attention

These next two chapters discuss the two most important principles I know for raising children: (1) Pay attention to good behavior and punish bad behavior briefly. Behavior of any kind will not continue long without attention. (2) There is more to discipline than lectures and punishment.

Attention, Please!

Nothing happens or continues to happen without some type of payoff or reward. Attention is the most powerful of all the payoffs. Most of us, adults and children alike, thrive on attention.

Imagine trying to talk with someone who is clearly not listening to you. In fact, she is carrying on a conversation with someone else: no shared eye contact, no responsive head-nodding, no smiles. She is not even facing you. How long will you continue talking with her? Probably not very long! It is almost impossible to continue a conversation with someone who does not respond in any way.

Imagine calling a "hello" across the street to an acquaintance. Your acquaintance glances briefly in your direction, and then looks away and continues walking without responding. You are very likely to be hurt. "How could he be so rude?" "What did I do to him the last time we met?" "Maybe he didn't recognize me." All sorts of explanations will run through your head. But you are very unlikely to continue a one-sided greeting. In the absence of any attention, you stop.

Behavior, even when it is bad behavior, will continue if it receives attention. How many times have we parents remarked: "The more I get after her the worse she gets?" Often we follow up this comment with an exasperated explanation: "She's just doing it to get attention." We *know* what the problem is and we know we are worsening matters by focusing on the misbehavior. We just don't know another way to handle the situation.

If being bad necessitates punishment, then being good deserves equal time. You can call it a bribe if you wish. But when people, big or little, do something worthwhile and nice, some sort of recognition or applause, whatever you call it, is appreciated.

There are many ways to reward behavior. Time and attention are the simplest, most important ways. When Dad sits with his son in the basement watching him hammer a makeshift boat, he is giving his time to reward woodworking. When mother asks about the details of a school success, she is paying attention.

Catching the Children in the Act

Parents must be very careful how they use their time and attention. As much as possible, they need to subtract attention from bad behavior and give it to the good. Ideally, parents need to catch their kids in the act—of being good. *That's* the time to pay attention.

For example, sometimes Mom and Dad become overwhelmed by all the trouble their son Johnny is in. "What are we going to do with that Johnny?" Dad asks. He and Mom are reviewing Johnny's latest escapade, added to a long list of misbehaviors.

Right at this point Dad and Mom need to take an equivalent inventory of all that is good about Johnny.

"Nothing," growls Mom. Her answer is a good indication why parents in this situation need to start thinking positively. They are in the rut of attending to their child's faults, but not his positive behavior. So Johnny may be misbehaving to get attention.

His parents should take an inventory of Johnny's good characteristics, such as he does a good job loading the dishwasher when he does it. Then when Johnny displays this behavior, they must pay attention to it, for instance, by saying to him "You're the best kitchen helper I have." If his parents can think of no particular achievements or even good characteristics, they might note some unconditional or neutral items. "He's our fourth grader." "He looks cute in his Superman t-shirt." Hugs and praise can be given for no reason at all. The silent message is "You don't have to be a bad boy to get attention."

The Power of Attention

You get more of any behavior you track. Industry knows this. Industry knows that whenever stats are kept on a behavior, the behavior will increase. Count assembly line products made in an hour and they will increase. Record consecutive days on time, days without absence and the higher attendance rate will increase.

Good coaches know this phenomenon. Whether noting miles run, laps swum, time spent lifting weights or practices attended, more is achieved by counting and keeping track. Moreover, if the coach gets after the runner for the miles not run, nags the swimmer for falling short, complains about weights not lifted or practices missed, the coach will get more of the same. Good coaches know it is far wiser to keep track of good plays than errors, to count hits rather than strikes, touchdowns rather than fumbles.

Why, then, do parents keep such careful track of mistakes?

Why is it that with our child's every wrong move or

mishap, our mouths shift into gear? Perhaps because our lectures sound so good, at least to us. We offer such great reasons for behaving. The problem is that we are offering them at the wrong time. We are giving the lecture (and the attention) at the moment of *mis*behavior. We need to reverse this habit, and learn to respond at the right time, when we are getting the *good* behavior we want.

One parent in my class objected. "I'm not going to bribe my child. He should be good simply because that's the right thing to do. He shouldn't have to have some reward." I responded, "Then why do you bribe him with your attention for being bad?"

Children, like all people, turn toward attention as flowers and their leaves turn toward the sunshine. Have you ever watched a nature film shot in slow sequence photography, capturing the activity of a single flower through the whole day? The flower points toward the sun constantly, following it across the sky from east to west. We are all like that with attention. Attention is our sunshine. We want, need, crave some response from others.

Avoiding Secondary Gain

Although there are other ways to discipline, punishment is sometimes necessary. When a parent punishes a child, the punishment must carry with it an absolute minimum of attention. Otherwise, the punishment will contain secondary gain for the child.

Punishment is primarily painful. Parents hope that pain will deter future misbehavior. The time the punishment takes and thereby the attention that comes from it, however, may provide a secondary gain. Unfortunately, the punishment may then become a perverted reward and, hence, a child will misbehave again to get the attention.

If you use punishment, strip any positive factors from it. Good punishment has qualities designed to guarantee a minimum of reward or gain for the child.

Qualities of Good Punishment

Good punishment is *brief.* Get it over with quickly. Long lectures are not brief. Nagging is not brief. Grounding is not brief. Hollering out the window for your four-year-old to come in is not brief. If the child won't come in, call once and then go get her. The more time the punishment takes, the more a reward factor is involved.

Good punishment is *immediate.* Telling a child to "Wait until your father comes home" is not immediate. Forbidding the movie on the coming Saturday for a misbehavior on the previous Tuesday is not immediate. If you must punish a misbehavior, do it at once. Mete out justice on the spot. Delaying the punishment or prolonging it provides too much attention and may encourage the behavior further.

Good punishment is *effective.* It works. Don't continue to shout louder or punish harder if you are not getting what you want. Stop what you are doing and try something else. Continuing a punishment that has no effect may cause the child increasing pain, but it is also giving more time and attention to the very behavior you want to eliminate. Furthermore, recognize that you cannot control certain behaviors. Eating, learning and sleeping are under the child's control. Many problems in these three areas originated in misguided parental attempts to make an issue of them. Punishment is rarely effective with eating, learning and sleeping.

Good punishment is *consistent.* You must mean what you say and stick to it day after day. If you make a promise or a threat, follow through. Mom and Dad need to back each other up. Otherwise, the child has a legitimate gripe: "It isn't fair! Mom let me do it." The intended discipline then becomes an argument game with lots of rewarding attention.

Consistency is especially difficult when a divorce has split the family because parents often disagree on child-rearing issues. However, they *must* work it out. The fact that they don't get along cannot be a complete obstacle. Although they are divorced as husband and wife, they cannot divorce as mother and father. In a split family situation, where the children live with one custodial parent, the children will often use this "gripe" as a bargaining chip: "Well, Dad says it's OK." Take a three-step approach to this tactic. First, check with Dad to see if he really does permit the behavior. Then, try to work out with him an agreed-upon response. And finally, if Dad won't agree, stick to your rules. Say: "That's fine when you're with Dad, but when you're with me, these are the rules."

Good punishment is *nonverbal*. By that, I don't mean spanking. I mean keep your mouth shut. Lectures take too long and reward misbehavior. Go get a child who won't come in. Separate combatants by putting them in different rooms. Grab the soccer player in the kitchen and hold onto him for a few moments. Pick up your daughter at her friend's house after curfew. The important thing is to concentrate on compliance rather than on your lecture or explanation. Get it done. Be effective with as little secondary gain as possible.

Ignoring Is Not Doing Nothing

Punishment is not the ideal discipline and certainly should not be the sole form of discipline. Ignoring a child's misbehavior is another option for parents, one that is frequently misunderstood. If you want a certain behavior to stop, ignore it. A child would rather have the behavior criticized or punished than ignored. Behavior that does not get attention tends to fade away.

Behavior that is ignored may disappear more slowly than behavior that is punished, but when the undesirable behavior is gone, it is gone for good. Indeed, psychologists say it has been extinguished. You do not want to extinguish the child, however, just the behavior. Planned ignoring is a negative response of non-reinforcement, non-attention, non-time, non-everything. All this negativism is aimed at the undesirable behavior. The *child* should never be ignored. She needs to be given attention, perhaps lots of it, not for bad behavior, but for the wonderful person she is. To let a child know he is loved, to notice the many good things the child does, to compliment far more than to criticize—these are the most important and satisfying aspects of parenting.

Planned ignoring requires that parents carefully target the behavior they wish to eliminate. Planned ignoring can be directed at any behavior that does not have to be stopped immediately. The purpose, of course, is to subtract all attention, and then trust that the misbehavior cannot continue in a vacuum.

Imagine that you came into my office with an outrageous hairstyle, one so blatant it practically demanded notice. Your hair was dyed orange with green streaks and swept up over a canary cage on top of your head. In the cage was a live, singing canary.

I might marvel: "Wow, what an interesting and outrageous hairdo. You look like an actress. Where'd you ever get that idea? You sure have some guts."

Or I might exclaim: "I can't believe you'd come into my office like that! Your hair looks awful. It's a disgrace. How can we talk with that stupid canary chirping. You should be ashamed of yourself! Who do you think you are?"

Or suppose I entirely ignored your hairdo, never said a word, just went on with the interview as if there were nothing unusual about your hair. Which of these three responses would make you least likely to come into my office again with such a hairdo?

Clearly, ignoring your hairdo is the best way to stop you. Why would you go to all that trouble again when I didn't even notice it? In responses one and two, on the other hand, you received a lot of attention. Even when the attention was negative (the second response), you still can return home with a puckish smile on your face thinking: "I had fun today. I really gave Dr. Kenny a hard time. Boy was he irritated."

However, ignoring doesn't work with behaviors that carry their own "rewards." Drugs, fast cars, sex and other behaviors with a high level of excitement or pleasure fantasies attached to them are rewarded without parental attention. But planned ignoring is a very good strategy for behaviors that thrive on parental attention, that seem geared to "get mother's goat."

Other Rewards

Attention, of course, is not the only reward, just the simplest and most ever-present. There are other ways to reward behavior.

Touch is an effective reinforcer. A "high-five" is an athlete's reward for a good effort. The teacher who touches the shoulders of an active first-grader in his seat may be encouraging sitting-in-your-seat behavior.

Praise is a mixed bag. It rewards, but it carries a subtle pressure to keep up the performance. It is not as effective as time, attention and touch.

Candy, pop, cake and cookies are sometimes used as rewards. The sugar content of these foods, however, might make you unhappy with your child's resulting behavior. Some alternatives might be fresh vegetables, popcorn or fruits.

The chance to learn can also be a reward for desirable behavior. Learning to play a musical instrument can be a reward. The child may welcome drawing lessons, working with tools (under adult supervision, of course), building models or working with clay. Learning to drive is important to older teens.

Toys are an obvious reward. One parent had a grab bag of small toys from which the child could select when things went well. Valued by most small children are cars, dolls, games, bicycles and many other items.

Excursions can be eagerly earned. They might include a ride in the car, going to work with Mom or Dad, going shopping with Mom or Dad or visiting with grandparents. How about a visit to the seashore, a train ride, an airplane ride, going out to dinner with Mom and Dad, visiting a friend, visiting a new city, visiting a museum or even taking a walk in the woods hunting for frogs, birds or leprechauns?

Entertainment is always popular. Going to a movie, watching a favorite TV program, listening to a special record or putting on a play or puppet show for parents can be a reward for good behavior.

Sports and games are attractive. Playing ball with Mom or Dad, swimming, bike riding, skating, horseback riding, ping-pong and fishing can all be used. Table games like chess or checkers are also popular. Believe it or not, helping around the house can be rewarding. Some children are eager to set the table, dust, make the beds, paint a room, do minor repairs and run errands. Baking cookies, picking flowers (even when unasked) and working in the garden may also be a treat. Older children usually see these as chores, but younger ones welcome the time with Mom or Dad.

Playing with friends, going to Scouts and having friends over may be special bonuses. Staying up past bedtime, caring for a pet and having a party are also worth working for, not to mention earning the use of the car, getting new clothes, putting on makeup or going to a beauty parlor. The objects and activities used as rewards can be as varied as the ages and interests of the children.

Rewards are like gold stars given to let our children know we value what they are doing. Time and attention are at the core. They tell our children they are special people.

Attention Techniques Applied

A Jealous Four-Year-Old

A mother was breast-feeding her infant. Meanwhile, her four-year-old began to remove the good crystal from the cabinet. Mother was frustrated and helpless. She was about to yell out, when it occurred to her that her four-year-old was being naughty because he was jealous. So she called him to her and explained how she had nursed him when he was a baby. She did not mention the crystal but enlisted his help caring for the baby. He got a dry diaper for her and fed the baby while she drew bath water. The misbehavior was forgotten because the mother had diverted her son into positive behavior and paid attention to that good behavior.

Teaching the ABCs: Accentuate the Positive

A father was trying to teach his first-grade daughter the alphabet. She came home from school with an unsatisfactory report card because she could not get the jumbled up "elemenopee" part. Father made the mistake of drilling her for three days on the part she had wrong. She got worse. Finally, he asked her to repeat the part she knew several times and he acted pleased. He let the difficult part go. After a few days he was amazed when she blurted out "L-M-N-O-P" correctly. They had not practiced it. The father had wisely changed his attention from the non-learning to the learning. The child, unconsciously recognizing how to receive attention, responded by learning the alphabet.

The Great Homework Battle

The great homework battle is a nightly five-hour encounter between parent and child. The parent tries to find out the assignment and see that it is completed and turned in the next day. The child tries to hide the assignment, stay lost until bedtime and generally resist any parental effort to get the homework done.

The first step is to know the assignments. Often parents are unable to get their children to bring the assignments home regularly. Even if they do, they cannot be sure that they have them all or that they are getting the truth.

If this is your frustration, try getting the homework assignments directly from the school. Either the homeroom teacher or school counselor should be able to provide them.

Usually the counselor will make a list of your child's daily classes and leave a space for each teacher to write in the day's assignment. Your child can present this list to each teacher after class, then bring the completed sheet to the counselor or bring it directly home, whichever works best.

Next, you and your child can select a homework time. One hour is enough, but you need to specify which hour. This prevents homework from becoming an all-evening contest. State that homework is expected only during a certain hour, perhaps 8:00 to 9:00 p.m. Then, pick a place for the homework to be done. Most anywhere except in front of the TV would be acceptable.

Finally, if your child is in place during the designated time with book and eyes open, he is doing his homework. He should receive some recognition or reward.

At this point, you've done your best. You cannot force learning to occur, but you can see that your child observes time and place. Then check daily with your child to see whether he has completed the daily home assignments. You might also want to check weekly with your child's teachers or counselor to confirm that the assignments are being turned in.

Keep a chart on your child's success. Give a point for every fifteen minutes at the designated time and place for homework. Also give a point for each home assignment completed. Make the points worth some small reward, such as so many points earn so much late time (time allowed to stay out *past* curfew), money or surprise gifts.

This is a positive way to get more homework. The designated time allows you to avoid the school-to-bed nagging. The designated place allows you to reward what you can actually observe. Checking with the teacher allows you to circumvent lying and forgetting. Success gets the attention. The battle is over.

A First-Grade Runaround: Targeting the "In" Seat

Here's a typical scenario. I am frequently called to school to help with overly active first-graders, especially those who like to run around the classroom. The teacher complains that Bobby is out of his seat all the time. I sit in the back of the room and observe for about half an hour. I have never seen a child out of his seat all the time, usually only about half of the time. The worst I have ever seen was about eighty percent of the time. I am sure, however, that it seems like *all* the time to the teacher.

This is what I hear. As Bobby leaves his seat, his teacher starts: "Bobby, please return to your seat. Remember how you promised me this morning before class? You said you would try...."

"Bobby!" (louder) "Stop running around. If everyone ran around the class when he felt like it, how could I teach? It would be a madhouse."

"Bobby!" (louder still) "Do you want me to call your mother again? Remember, I called her last week and she came into school and she was very angry with you. Shall I call...."

"Bobby!" (louder and more rapidly) "I'm going to send you to the principal's office. We have permission to rap your knuckles. Remember yesterday when that happened and you cried all day?"

Finally, screaming: "Bobby!!! Jesus died on the cross so children would obey their teachers and parents, and he had to hang there thinking that you don't even care."

The teacher has gone from a simple please all the way to the ultimate moral admonition. And does it work? Obviously not, or she would not have called me. She even tells me why it doesn't work.

"The more I get after Bobby, the worse he gets."

Then she adds the reason. "He's just doing it to get attention."

So I tell her: "Then keep quiet."

She replies: "I can't."

"Why not?" I ask.

"Because he'll run all around the classroom," she answers.

"He's doing that now," I comment.

She laughs. "I guess that the real reason is that my mouth is tied to his feet. When his feet start, so does my mouth."

I laugh, too, at her honesty. And I admit that ignoring his out-of-seat behavior is only half the solution.

"One more step," I say. "When he's in his seat, I want you to touch him. Tap his shoulder. Tousle his hair. Pat his back. No praising, just touch."

In most cases, this simple plan results in one hundred percent in-seat behavior within one week. If not, then I suggest that in addition to touching the child, the teacher talk with him briefly, but only when he is in his seat. What the teacher has done very simply is to reverse the behavior she pays attention to. She only paid attention to Bobby when he was out of his seat. Now she only touches and talks to him when he is in his seat. And it works.

The Curfew Switch

Both parents came with Sandy. Sandy was sixteen; the family was referred by the probation department because

Sandy had run away. In fact, Sandy had run away three times and had not come home earlier than 3 a.m. for one month. Her parents felt Sandy was uncontrollable and they were ready to give up. "Find a foster home or an institution," they said.

I saw Sandy alone. She was crying. She did not want to leave her home. I asked her what she wanted most. "More freedom," she said. Like many teenagers, she felt that her parents were being too restrictive.

While the wishes of parents and teen at first appeared contradictory, I had an idea. "What about a bargain?" I asked. "Would you be willing to enter into a behavior contract with your parents?"

Sandy was interested and asked what I meant. I replied that she would have to agree to a curfew. In return for following her curfew, her parents would award her one bonus point each night she was in on time. Each bonus point would be worth fifteen minutes of late time.

Her parents were interested, too. We negotiated a ten o'clock curfew for school nights, and eleven o'clock on Friday and Saturday nights. After some discussion, we added a penalty for being late. Sandy agreed to perform one hour of hard work the next day for each fifteen minutes she was late before she went out again. We typed up the contract and made up a chart to keep track of the nights she came home on time.

Although her parents were at first skeptical, the contract and chart worked like a miracle. Sandy came home on time for thirteen straight nights. Then on the fourteenth night, a Saturday night, as Sandy left, she rather flippantly told her father: "So long Daddy-o. See you at 2:15." (That was her eleven o'clock curfew plus thirteen bonus points.)

Dad, however, exploded. "No, you don't," he shouted. Sandy left anyway and ran away again.

Two days later, back in my office, we were able to straighten out the conflict. Dad argued: "No daughter of mine is going to stay out after 2 a.m."

Mom shot back: "Your daughter never came home before 3 a.m. for a whole month. Then we got something working and you blew it."

After some more talking, we all came to a better understanding of what a contract meant.

Sandy never had to leave her home for a foster home. After two more years of better-than-most adherence to her curfew, Sandy graduated from high school and went to college. Her parents had learned, by setting a clear penalty in advance, to give minimal attention to curfew violation. At the same time, they rewarded her coming home on time with a bonus. It worked and they saved their daughter. The trick was to reverse their strategy and give attention, not to coming home late, but to being on time.

Counting the Miles

Pay attention to the behavior you want. Stop giving lectures when you confront misbehavior. This simple principle works just as well with adults as with children. Imagine the smoker who goes two weeks without a cigarette. No one says a word. Then he lights one up and his friend says: "Hey, John, what's this? I thought you stopped smoking."

Or what about the lady who goes on a diet. She watches her intake and loses six pounds, and doesn't hear a word of praise from anyone. Then one day she reaches for a chocolate and her husband teases her: "Can't restrain yourself, can you? I thought you were serious about that diet."

As I said earlier, I collapsed fifteen years ago and was told to start a regular moderate exercise program. My oldest son, Joe, was a long-distance runner. "That's all right, Dad," he said. "Run." He bought me running shorts and shoes, and gave me a pep talk about running for my life and health.

I started out with great enthusiasm but stalled about three weeks later. My legs hurt. My chest hurt. I didn't have enough time. There was always an excuse.

Joe offered to run with me. I value being a father, so that suggestion was highly motivating. What father would refuse to run with his son? That episode also lasted about three weeks before I petered out amid a plethora of excuses.

Then my wife started running. That did it. I was born in an age when men were the competitors and girls were the cheerleaders. The worst thing that ever happened to me in my life was in the seventh grade when a girl named Edwina caught me from behind and washed my face in the snow. Oh, the shame! What if my wife, Mary, were to beat me. On went the shoes and shorts again and off I went...for another three weeks. And, again, my motivation waned.

Run for your health. Run to be a good father. Run for your machismo. All good reasons, but all came at the wrong time. Hard to believe, but all these strategies were actually rewarding my non-running.

Then my son, Joe, changed his approach. "Have you run yet, Dad?" he asked when I got home from work. "Not yet," I answered. He walked over and wrote a little zero in the upper left-hand corner of the date on our kitchen calendar.

"What's that?" I asked. "Those are your miles," he said non-committally. "I'm keeping track."

The third day I walk-jogged a mile just to see what it would look like on the calendar. I did manage another mile that week and five miles the second week. Joe kept counting. I ran fourteen miles the third week. And I'm still keeping track, still running. On my fiftieth birthday, I ran the Chicago Marathon.

How did it happen? My son stopped multiplying arguments and started counting miles. You get what you notice. He got the miles.

Hence, parents need to design their disciplinary strategy to target good behavior rather than bad. The ideal is to be able to reward the opposite of the bad. If Bobby is in his seat, he can't be out of it. If Sandy is home on time, she can't be late. Ignore the bad when possible, no matter how sensible and reasonable your lecture. And pay attention to the good when it happens.

CHAPTER FOUR

Discipline Is More Than Punishment

P unishment is not discipline. It is not even the chief ingredient in discipline. In fact, punishment, despite its common use, is often not even very good discipline because it does not work well to obtain the desired result. Discipline includes many more techniques than punishment. If you prefer a mathematical formula, you might express it as D>P.

Discipline is the total character-molding of the child through love, example, praise and attention for good behavior, and ignoring and punishment for bad behavior. Punishment provides a short-term, temporary deterrent. Experts generally agree that punishment alone does not eliminate bad behavior permanently.

A list of common punishments will make some of the drawbacks clear. Spanking may induce conformity out of fear, but the fear may interfere with the child-parent bond of trust and affection. Scolding is rarely wise because it takes too long and, thereby, provides too much attention to the negative behavior. Isolation for an extended period is a good way to end bickering and fighting, but it deprives the child of the chance to express herself properly and to learn to get along with others. Withdrawal of love can be extremely effective, but it hurts at the core of the child's self. Denial of food can also be effective. The problem is that because children sometimes associate food with love, the denial of food becomes, to the child, a denial of the parent's love. Withdrawing privileges and limiting a child to his room can work well with a teenager. An undesired side effect, however, is that the teen may spend more time longing for escape than meditating on improving his behavior.

To understand more fully the drawbacks of these punishments, imagine receiving them yourself. How does it feel to have privileges taken away? Imagine being sent to your room in disgrace. What do you feel when someone keeps you from eating because of something you did? How does it feel when someone yells at you for ten minutes in front of everyone else in your family?

As a primary means of behavior control, punishment can be indicted on four counts. Punishment negates the person. It fails to offer a blueprint for virtue. It becomes less effective as children grow older. It provides valued time and attention for the wrong behavior.

Too often children are subjected to a barrage of what's wrong with them.

> "Who left the front door open?"

> "Is Charlie late again?"

> "What's the matter with that girl?"

Statements like these give the child a negative self-image. The child confronted with parents who are constantly scolding, yelling, moralizing and spanking her will learn either that she is a bad character or that her parents are to be avoided.

Punishment, with its focus on misbehavior, fails to tell a child what he should be doing. Somewhere in their disciplinary efforts, parents must indicate, not through a sermon, but through example, time and attention, what they would like their child to do and be.

Punishment is less effective with older children because parents control less of their significant environment. Indeed, often they are too big to spank. A parent's harsh words are no longer devastating since teens can muster support from their friends. Sending teens to their rooms can be just what they want, an occasion to play the stereo loud. If the punishment is seen by the teenager as severe enough, she may even muster the courage to run away.

The most serious indictment of punishment, as we have already discussed, is that it may encourage the very behavior parents are attempting to eliminate. By focusing on the undesirable behavior, parents are providing secondary gain. Although the primary thrust of punishment is always meant to be unrewarding and painful, too often the secondary gain outweighs the primary painfulness.

Two of the more popular punishments used by parents are spanking and grounding. If they worked well, parents would not have to use them so often. Yet despite the fact that they are relatively ineffective, parents continue to use them. Why? Probably because they hurt. But hurting someone is not necessarily effective. The key question parents need to keep asking is: Does punishment work?

Spanking

I am against child abuse. I am not necessarily against spanking. A simplistic view that states physical punishment never should be used fails to consider that verbal and mental abuse by parents and teachers can be more devastating than physical abuse. It is also incorrect because sometimes spanking is not abusive but appropriate.

I object to the mother in the store who pounds on her three-year-old out of frustration. I am firmly opposed to the father who, in righteous anger, beats up his fourteen-year-old son who has just been caught smoking. Yet I have seen verbal attacks by parents and teachers that were far more destructive—subtle criticism, ridicule, put-downs, insulting and mean comments. A sharp-tongued adult can destroy the self-image, the very soul of a child without even touching that child.

There is a difference between proper spanking and violence. I am not for physical or verbal violence (striking in fury, anything that leaves marks, forty-five minute lectures that rip a child's soul to threads). A spanking is not a beating. It is a quick slap. And it can, in fact, be a legitimate response to what Lawrence Kohlberg describes as Stage One Morality in child development.

According to Kohlberg, moral readiness develops through as many as six stages, depending upon intelligence, the ability to abstract, maturity and experience. Stage One is the level of pure self-interest where the child seeks pleasure and avoids pain. At the stage one level, then, the spanking (a quick slap) can be a simple touch-communication and a painful one. A good example is a two-year-old who starts to toddle across the street. A verbal "NO" plus a quick spank on the leg is a great improvement over a lecture and long explanation.

We know from psychology that adult time and attention are major rewards. Long lectures and nagging can actually be perceived by the child as rewards. They encourage the very behavior they are supposed to eliminate. Therefore, a spanking must be brief and immediate to hold minimal reward value for the child.

However, because adults can lose their tempers, I suggest three simple safeguards when spanking:

1) Never spank in anger.

2) Never spank without a witness. This is as good a rule for parents as it is for teachers. Ideally, a sibling or spouse should be nearby.

3) Don't spank after age four, unless the child is behaving (misbehaving) at a preschool level. By this I mean impulsive, uninhibited, unplanned behavior. Never spank or strike a teen.

Grounding

Most, if not all, teens resent being grounded for an indefinite period. As one teen wrote me: "My parents have grounded me forever or, as my father put it, 'until your attitude improves.' I am a high school junior girl and I hate being grounded. I know I had some punishment coming because I stayed out too late, and I sassed both my parents. But now I am missing all my friends, school events, everything. My attitude is getting worse. I want to run away and live somewhere else."

Some parents feel grounding *is* a good punishment precisely because their teenagers hate it so much. Causing pain and distress, however, is not the primary purpose of parental punishment. A punishment is only good if it works to *change* behavior.

Grounding is a poor punishment because it fails to accomplish its objective. There are better ways to get teens home on time and speaking pleasantly. Further, indefinite grounding tends to cause a lot of continuing disharmony between parents and teen.

Indefinite grounding is poor discipline for several psychological reasons. Mainly, it lasts too long, giving too much attention over too long a period to misbehavior. Behavior that gets attention of any kind continues. "Indefinite" does not put a time limit on the punishment; it is too vague. How can you judge when "your attitude improves"? It is better to set a specific date that the grounding will be over and to assign some tasks the teen must do to show "attitude improvement."

Finally, grounding is poor discipline because it deprives the teen of something good and worthwhile. Relationships and extracurricular school events are an important part of growing up.

There are alternatives to grounding. Why not assign extra chores? For example, for every fifteen or thirty minutes the teen is late, he must scrub floors, wash cabinets, clean windows and so on for a certain designated period of time.

Why not take a positive approach and reward the teen for good behavior? Perhaps you can give him use of the family car if he comes home on time. Follow the example set by Sandy and her parents. Each night she is home by curfew, she earns one half hour of car time. Or she gets late time on certain nights for keeping curfew. In this way the attention goes to the good behavior rather than the bad.

Talk with your teen. Let him know what you want and what you are willing to give in return. Listen to him. Tell him what you expect. Somewhere, you may be able to strike a bargain that is more effective and less disagreeable then indefinite grounding.

Love Unconditionally

The best preventive discipline is love. If a child has done something bad and her parents can find little that is attractive in her behavior, they can love her simply because her name is Sarah and her hair is brown.

"How's my second daughter?"

"How's my third-grader?"

As I said in Chapter Two, this is unconditional love, neither earned nor merited. Parents demand nothing. The love penetrates past the child's behavior to her person. Her parents love and accept her with all her faults. As one child-care expert said, it means to live with your child so that she is deeply and quietly glad she is who she is.

Home itself should be the center of unconditional love. Home should be a place of refuge for children, a place where all family members can come to lick their wounds. Home should be the one place where you won't be put down, where you can expect a smile and a pat on the back, not because you accomplished or failed to accomplish great things, but because this is the place where you belong, your safe harbor. Children need that place of sanctuary.

Unconditional love is more than a preventive. It is the foundation for self-acceptance and for learning to love others. It is critical to be loved for yourself, to learn that life is a come-as-you-are party and that it is OK to be *you*.

What wife has not been surprised to receive an unexpected gift of flowers or candy just because "I love you"? What husband has not warmed to an unsolicited touch or kiss from his wife? All of us need unconditional love with no strings attached and no conditions to be met. We need straightforward spontaneous messages that say: "Glad to have you around. You're OK."

Nurturing love is most often shown babies. Touching skin-to-skin, singing, cooing, holding and all kinds of happy times spent with the baby are the ways this love is best expressed.

Although touch may decrease as the child grows older, touch can continue to express nurturing love for persons of all ages. Small gifts or favors and helping the child graciously, even at some inconvenience to oneself, are other expressions of nurturing love for the older child. Nurturing love is expressed by that person who is willing to go the extra mile simply because she cares. Everyone needs nurturing love in life.

For older children, allowances can be used as a way to express unconditional love. From kindergarten on, the child receives a modest amount of money just because he belongs. He does not have to earn it. The allowance is never taken away in punishment. The allowance comes to her as regularly as the sun rises.

Using allowance in this way has many advantages. Not only does the child get something of worth from his parents unconditionally, but also he is thereby spared having to go to them and beg for money every time he wishes to make a small purchase. Furthermore, with a guaranteed income that has no strings attached, the child can learn on his own how to use money, beginning with the important lesson: If you spend it, you no longer have it.

Parents can supplement the allowance with jobs that pay the child for work well done. But since in our culture money is often a way of showing love, the regular guaranteed allowance is recommended as an expression of unconditional love.

Another level of unconditional love is rapport, which involves mutual liking and respect. To establish rapport with one's children takes time and attention. There is no substitute for spending time with those we love. In fact, some psychologists use "time spent with" as an operational definition of "love."

To spend time simply enjoying the company of your children is essential for rapport. Let them show you their drawings, play their records for you. Teach them to drive and recognize the opportunity to be with them. Take an adolescent shopping, to a movie or athletic event. Play table and card games. Show home movies. Have a dinner party with your children. Look for ways to *enjoy* your children.

Good communication is still another way to express unconditional love. Perhaps one of the first things lovers say about their beloved is "he/she understands me." Children who feel their parents understand them will feel good about themselves and be less apt to misbehave.

Understanding is no accident. It is brought about by individual attention and active listening. Active listening means the constant attempt to echo and rephrase what the child has said until the child tells you that you understand.

Let's look at an example. Jeff comes home quiet and unsmiling.

"Hi, Jeff."

No answer.

"Bad day?"

"Yeah."

"It gets you down when things don't go the way you want."

"Yeah. The teacher made us do our papers over. The track coach zapped me for being late. I feel like quitting."

"Everything went wrong and you feel like quitting."

"Yeah. And another thing...."

Jeff then becomes more animated. Because his Dad gave no advice and made no judgment, a quiet and angry boy was able to share his feelings by putting them into words. The active listener who echoes, reflects and does nothing more will be perceived as understanding.

Feelings are important in communication. If parents are any good at listening, they will begin to hear the heart. Children should be allowed to express all their feelings, including the negative ones. Feelings like anger are not pleasant, but they are better expressed in words than in behavior. Besides, feelings arise unbidden in a child. She may be responsible for her actions but not for feelings she cannot help.

Sometimes children close themselves off from parents. Reaching out in quiet parental love may take some effort. The child who resists affection still needs it. Even the resistive child can often be reached when he is particularly happy, sad, angry, proud, scared or sick. Sit down to watch TV with him; walk up behind him and quietly rub his back, stating the obvious: "You seem very quiet"; put a little surprise—a chocolate kiss—under her pillow. All these gestures say to the child "It's OK if you're confused. If you feel like talking, I'm here for you." Try telling your child how you feel, "I feel lonesome and I'm wondering how you feel." Or, with a young child, tell a story something like this one: "Once there was a lonely little monkey who needed to talk to someone but couldn't and finally said to his mom, 'I don't know what to say' and his mom said, 'That's OK, I don't know what to say either.' And they hugged each other, happy to share their common stupidity."

Prevention Through Positive Planning

Some parents seem to be lucky. Everything works out. Other parents envy them and wish they too were so fortunate with their children. What appears to be luck may actually be good planning. These parents have probably arranged their homes and family lives so that discipline takes care of itself. They have worked to structure their environments in such a way that the discipline is built in.

Playtime

The first step in structuring for success is to let the child be himself as he grows. For the smaller child, this means childproofing the home to allow him to expend the energy of childhood without destroying the family heirlooms. Children are children and should be allowed the latitude of their age, with its problems and tasks. Of course, parental protection may be necessary occasionally to protect from real danger and to anticipate disasters. In addition, parents should plan positively for good behavior, provide learning and fun experiences to counter boredom and find constructive ways to channel the energy of childhood.

Childproofing a home is not enough, however. Homes need to be full of materials that invite activity and participation, chalkboards for drawing and writing, bulletin boards to hold messages and artwork. Some children get into mischief because they don't know what else to do. The wise parent prevents boredom in her child by providing learning and fun experiences appropriate to the child's age. Give a toddler a small cup of water with food coloring in it and let him paint old newspapers with a pastry brush. Paper used on one side and discarded by businesses can provide abundant, cheap drawing material. Plenty of crayons, marking pencils and paints of various kinds should be available. Children will draw and paint endlessly. As one mother put it: "The major decorative motif in our house is tape."

Ideal toys include blocks, construction sets, little plastic people, trucks, trains and potter's clay. Equally interesting are boxes, wrapping paper, sticks and string. Boxes can be stacked, hid in, used to carry other toys, drawn on and thrown at. Just make sure you remove any loose tape or staples from the boxes to prevent injury to your child.

Other favorite toys are pots and pans, dishes, sand, drawers, the magazine rack and the sink. The wise parent buys sturdy pots and pans, unbreakable dishes, selects the safer tools for the child to play with and dresses the child to play in the sand and gravel or at the sink. When engaged in such play, the child is not only learning about the world but is also channeling energy and curiosity in constructive ways.

The most popular play materials are simple but stimulating. They have few fine details and many uses. In contrast, modern advertising pressures parents to buy mechanical toys and fancy dolls with very limited functions. Children often lose interest quickly in these toys.

Older children like stereos, tape recorders, cameras, VCRs, telescopes and microscopes. Listen with your children to the records they enjoy. Let them tell you why they like the music. Teach them how to record their favorite tunes on a cassette, how to run the VCR, how to examine tissue under the microscope, how to use materials and appliances of all varieties, how to recognize the constellations. Spend an evening searching the sky for that special star or the Milky Way.

Even the much-maligned radio and television can be a healthy part of the family environment. Stop worrying about your child's taste in television and start some positive planning from the week's radio or television listings. Select for the week five programs that promise to be fun and educational for the family. Remind everyone. Make popcorn. Get in there yourself and watch with your children.

Games are popular with all ages. From the card game Go Fish with young children to the elaborate financial dealings of Monopoly®, most children welcome games with each other and with their parents. New card games and board games are introduced every year. Some become classics. Choose games according to the interests of the family. If you try a new game that is too confusing or uninteresting to appeal to everyone, give it away. There are too many good games to waste your time on a poor one.

Classic games from Africa and the Orient are now gaining popularity in the West. Frequently, they use simple materials in ways that are every bit as fascinating as our classic checkers and chess.

Mealtime

Are mealtimes a disaster, interrupted by latecomers and spiced by arguments?

"Why doesn't Tom have to eat his spinach?"

"You never get after Jan when she's late."

"I'm not hungry."

"Dad, tell Annie to shut her big mouth."

Parents can wage a constant battle to beg and plead for a quieter dinnertime or they can plan ahead for a pleasant mealtime.

Begin the meal with a short blessing or song. Take turns recounting the most important event of each member's day. Read something inspirational or something funny for the first few minutes. The beginning of the meal sets the tone for the rest of the meal. Surprisingly, children often enjoy a short reading at mealtime and, once they get used to this practice, they may miss it if it is omitted.

Plan to raise specific topics as the meal progresses. Share letters and news from relatives or family and friends. Announce upcoming plans and activities that concern all family members.

If your toddler keeps getting up and down from the table, let the child leave the table, rather than upset the rest of the family's meal. It's difficult to force a four- or five-year-old into the adult mode of sitting still in one place for thirty minutes. You can accommodate the child to the point of letting him leave the table, but don't allow him to have any more food until the next morning. Let hunger teach the importance of eating at mealtime. Remember the basic reason for the meal is not to teach the child to sit still for thirty minutes but to learn to eat a nutritious meal.

Whatever your family situation, keep in mind this basic principle: Mealtime should be a joyous time and one of good nourishment.

Bedtime

Bedtime can provoke undesirable behavior in the form of rebellion, procrastination and some horseplay after the child is supposed to be in bed and asleep. Again, why not anticipate this reaction and do something to make bedtime attractive?

Bedtime can be preceded by a transition period to calm down. Rituals such as drinks of water, prayers and heart-to-heart parent-child talks serve this function. There is no better time to talk things over seriously and lovingly with your child than just before bed.

Reading a story is the most popular of all bedtime rituals. "Once upon a time...." and the parent and child are off on a trip through the woods with Little Red Riding Hood, down Mulberry Street with Dr. Seuss, to Never-Never Land with Peter Pan or into the Hundred Acre Woods with Winnie the Pooh. Heaven help you if you try to vary even one little word in the child's favorite story. The child will remind you: "That's not the way it goes!"

Indeed, parents can even tell their own stories. Children love to hear stories about when Dad or Mom were little. All children are fascinated by ghost stories (although that may not be the best bedtime subject for a sensitive, easily scared youngster). One father makes up a nightly story about a family of monkeys named Wumps that live in a jungle. The monkeys have the same first names as his children, and they reside in a tree house with Daddy Gorilla and Mommy Chimpanzee. The little monkeys meet snakes and witch doctors, crocodiles and zoo collectors, but in general their life parallels that of their human counterparts.

The children love it and Dad is flattered to have such an appreciative audience.

Outdoor Activities and Family Trips

Many healthy activities take place outdoors. Family camping is a good introduction to basic living. Children learn how to build a fire, cook, put up a tent and arrange for sleep and other necessities in unusual places. In addition, by word and example, parents need to encourage other outdoor activities such as biking, swimming and jogging.

The family excursion, however, ranks high on most potential disaster lists. Sharon has to sit in the middle of the back seat and immediately accuses her brother of hogging all the air. Five miles down the road Ken announces he forgot his swimsuit. Teenager Tom wonders aloud why he has to go along in the first place. Mike wants to know when he gets to drive. Lisa wants to listen to the local rock station on the radio. Then the poking and pushing start.

The best defense is positive planning. The Petersons have five children. They plan their trips carefully. Every two hours they take a rest for snacks and bathroom breaks, and to change drivers. The older passengers rotate as driver, navigator and Master of Ceremonies (MC) for the youngsters. The MC's job is to maintain harmony within the car.

The MC may read aloud, play tapes on the car cassette player or initiate games, such as auto bingo, cards, portable checkers, the alphabet (watch road signs for words beginning with the A-B-Cs in order; the first one to Z wins) and counting cows on your side of the car (passing a lake drowns five and a cemetery kills all of them). The MC must plan the allotted two-hour recreation schedule in advance. The Petersons enjoy their family trips; they are active and noisy but organized.

Natural Consequences

Structuring so that desirable behavior occurs is the best strategy. But even in the best organized homes, a misact will slip through the preventive defenses now and then. Remembering, however, that actions have consequences can help parents stay out of the picture and let the natural consequences of the act do the disciplining.

For example, one child is friendly and helpful, and as a result, other children like her. So the child continues being friendly in order to be liked. Another child fails to attend all practice sessions of the track team and does poorly in competition. Hence, the consequences of the child's actions will often reward the good and extinguish the bad.

Despite the power of consequences, however, many parents intervene to protect their children from the results of their actions. Johnny has an auto accident due to carelessness, so Dad buys him another car to replace the loss. Susie loses her money on the way to the carnival, so Mom gives her more. Bob gets in trouble at school for truancy, and his parents use legal loopholes to help him avoid the customary suspension.

Parents love their children, sometimes in an overly protective way. They are reluctant to let them learn the lessons of their behavior. Perhaps parents fear the child will not love them if they do not protect the child from loss and pain.

Parents do their children a disservice when they overprotect them. The children need to learn that their parents have enough confidence in their ability to cope to let them experience the consequences, allowing for the appropriate precautions or "safety nets."

In other words, in cases where physical safety is involved, the parent must protect the child from natural consequences. Other times a parent might decide that the consequences will be more severe than the offense warrants. Thus the parent will remind Junior to turn in his

Little League application. The reminder may not cure his forgetfulness, but it will save a disappointed, and very active, youngster from sitting in the stands for the entire baseball season.

Likewise, in a busy city neighborhood the parent should either remind the child at night to put his bike away or put the bike away himself. A stolen bicycle may be too high a price for leaving it outside. The parent who stands back and allows overly severe consequences to discipline the child is only expressing parental anger toward the child in a passive way.

Most situations, however, are less than severe and very amenable to letting the results do the discipline. The child who is late for meals can learn to prepare his own food and clean up afterward. Letting the child go hungry until the next mealtime is another appropriate natural consequence for coming late to dinner.

Does your child drag her feet in the morning and miss her ride to school? Let her walk or ride her bike. Is she then late for school? Let her stay after or experience whatever other penalty the school imposes on tardy students.

Does he forget things? Unless they are major items that will cause him to suffer for many days, let him forget them.

One of my favorite examples is about Doug who always forgot his lunch even though his mom reminded and nagged him. Often, she brought it to him at school. Then one day she stopped. Doug forgot again, had to borrow leftovers from the other kids and went a little hungry. He forgot his lunch once more. Now he never forgets it.

My least favorite is about the father who, upon finding out that his seventeen-year-old son had received a speeding ticket, lectured him unmercifully that speed kills, a car can be a dangerous weapon and drivers need to be responsible persons. The father then paid his son's ticket, or worse yet, pulled strings to get him off. It would have been far better for the father to be sympathetic about the high cost of speeding and let his son pay that cost. The ticket is a better motivator to slow down than the father's long lecture, and, father paying the ticket rewarded the bad behavior.

Natural consequences are just another name for life experience. Learning from one's actions is a lesson in which life is the teacher. Occasionally, life's teachings are too harsh, and the child must be protected. More often, however, life is a good and gentle teacher. Letting children face the consequences of their actions shows them that their parents have confidence in them. They no longer require complete protection. They can face life's lessons and handle them because, little by little, experience by experience, they are growing up.

Set a Good Example

Teaching and setting a good example can encourage good behavior and discourage the bad. Smoking, drinking, eating habits, exercise and attitudes toward religion are some areas where example counts.

Don't expect your child to be a nonsmoker if you smoke.

Don't expect your child not to overindulge in alcohol or drugs if you overindulge in liquor from time to time.

Don't expect your child to eat a balanced diet if you have a habit of indulging in rich foods or if you go to the other extreme and skip meals.

Don't expect your child to value exercise if your only exercise is getting up and down from the table and getting up from the sofa to turn on the TV remote control.

Don't expect your child to be religious if you do not attend church or if you ignore living your religious beliefs daily.

Lying: The Miranda Rule

When I ask parents what behavior they would most like to eliminate in their child's repertoire of misbehavior, lying heads the list.

"A betrayal of family trust," said one parent.

"How can you have good parent-child communication if you never know whether your child is telling the truth?"

Truth is a rather vague concept, especially to children. "What is truth?" asked Pontius Pilate (John 18:38). Exaggerations and omissions may seem perfectly legitimate to one person and be called a lie by another.

There is one time, however, when a lie is actually not a lie. If you are stopped by the police and accused of speeding, you may deny this. This is not a lie; it is a "not guilty" plea. Our Supreme Court has ruled that no one is obligated to confess or to incriminate oneself.[5] We parents need to grant this same right to our children. If we do so, much "lying" will be eliminated.

Children, like adults, "lie" to avoid trouble and to keep from getting caught. This tactic is more common with older children. At least we adults understand the motivation behind this kind of lying. The child is protecting his or her self-interest, a move we dislike because it is calculated and deliberate.

The best way to stop this kind of untruth is not to ask questions that require self-incrimination. Gather the evidence from other sources. Confront, accuse and punish children when necessary. But don't force them to tell on themselves.

Avoiding self-incrimination eliminates big battles about confessing and telling the truth. The parent no longer has to demand that the child confess, with dire threats if he does not or if he lies. Less attention is given to misbehavior

[3] In Miranda v. Arizona in 1966, the Supreme Court ruled that before any questioning begins, suspects in police custody must be informed of their right to remain silent, that anything they say may be used against them, and that they have the right to counsel.

and, at the same time, there is no temptation for the child to lie.

In summary, if you have reason to expect a lie, don't ask. Check the information through other sources.

Separating the Combatants

While the amount of fighting between brothers and sisters may vary, the occurrence of siblings fighting is universal. Bickering, complaining, hitting and accusing are facts of family life. Sometimes the fights can be ignored. When physical or mental harm is being done, or when the parent is frazzled and needs some peace, the fighting needs to be stopped. How do you stop a sibling squabble?

The worst way is to try to out-shout the rival factions. What parent has not yelled: "Shut up!" only to hear each side's innocence and the other's fault? Now, you, the parent, are yourself a combatant. That's no help.

Another no-win approach is to try to act as referee. "Let's get to the bottom of this," you offer. You are in for a long session, one designed to provide far too much attention to family feuds.

There is a much simpler way: Separate the combatants. Put them in a room apart, no arguments.

"You go to the kitchen and you go to the living room."

It's like a no-fault divorce. Neither side is to blame, but the fighting is stopped.

This simple strategy works. The desired outcome is obtained. The fighting is stopped with no further nonsense, no extra attention. The children learn that if fighting passes a certain point, it ends quickly and without punishment or fanfare.

Another version of this strategy is a game I call "Hugo." When fighting gets out of hand, one of the children is designated as Hugo, and Hugo ("you go") goes outside. The children can even take turns being Hugo.

Make the separation brief, perhaps only for a few

minutes, just long enough for the quarrel to be forgotten. If it begins again, separate them again.

Stopping the Noise

Noise is an ancient and universal family problem. Many ethnologies[5] of primitive hunting and gathering bands have reported that most of the complaints in the bands concerned too much noise in the hut next door. Things have not changed that much. Today's parent complains about constant bickering, shouting and loud stereos. How do you restore quiet, or at least dampen the noise pollution?

Certainly not by trying to out-shout the noise with ear-blasting commands of your own to "TURN THAT DOWN!" or "SHUT UP!" These reactions only make you part of the game and one of the noisemakers yourself.

If your children can stand the noise, but you can't, try earplugs. After all, you're the one having the problem. If earplugs solve the problem, why not?

Most parents, however, don't want to wear earplugs. If you're one, then separate the noisemakers. Most child noise is produced in groups, in concert. Use the techniques suggested in "Separating the Combatants." That may solve the problem without a lecture and undue parental attention.

"Silver Whistle" is a game we invented for quiet. A dime store whistle hangs in each room. Anyone who feels overwhelmed by the noise may blow the whistle. Everyone who is then quiet until the whistle blows again (usually in one to three minutes) receives a food treat. It works. And it is more fun and positive than shouting an angry and frustrated command.

---

[4] Ethnology is a branch of anthropology that deals primarily with the comparative and analytical study of a culture.

Going and Getting:
A Parent's Collection Agency Strategy

Mother's face appears at the window. "Susie, come in," she calls nicely. Three-year-old Susie does not respond. For the next fifteen minutes, Mother calls every minute or two with the same result. Finally, frustrated, Mother comes storming out, spanks Susie and complains to all the neighbors that children don't mind like they used to.

If only Susie's mother had spared herself and Susie all that calling and resulting frustration. Call her once. If Susie does not come, go and collect her. Carry her if necessary. There is no need to be unpleasant or to spank. Yet the message to Susie is very clear: When Mother calls, you come in, one way or another. It works with far less secondary gain than the prolonged hollering.

A similar but more serious incident occurred about five years ago at a New Year's Eve party. It was about 11:15 p.m. and I noticed that our host, Bill, was rather anxiously looking at his watch. "What's the matter, Bill?" I asked. "It's my daughter, Sandy," he replied. "She was due at eleven tonight and she's not here yet. Usually, she's very good about curfew, but tonight I'm a little worried."

Sandy was sixteen and Bill's oldest daughter. Meanwhile, another guest, John, joined us.

Bill continued: "Earlier today, Sandy asked me if she could go to a New Year's Eve party at the Henleys'. I asked if there would be adults at home. When she said she didn't know, I said I would call. She screamed at me that I couldn't do that and stomped out. Later, at six, she left saying I'd better think up a good punishment for her. Sandy's like that, a lot of mouth but usually obeys. Frankly, though, this time may be different."

John could not restrain himself. "I can't believe you let your daughter talk to you like that. If my daughter ever behaved like that to me, she'd learn very quickly that she'd better show me more respect. My daughter is at the Henley party, and she knows if she's not home by eleven, she'll be very sorry." John went on to say Bill was far too permissive, and raised his glass to toast "Bill the wimp."

Shortly thereafter, Bill disappeared. He returned to the party at 11:45 with Sandy. I couldn't resist this wonderful chance to learn something about parenting, so I quickly went over to Bill. So did John.

"What happened?" I asked.

"Well, I'm not sure I did right," Bill volunteered. "But I got her home."

He went on: "I got within a block of the Henleys' and you could tell by the music that no adult was present: heavy metal, loud enough to wake the dead. Anyway, I knocked on the door. A young man answered and I walked in without being asked, telling him to notify Sandy that her father was here. He hesitated a minute, then shouted: 'Sandy, your old man's here.'

"Sandy came into the living room very angry. She was shouting: 'I can't believe you spoiled our party. You have embarrassed me forever in front of my friends. If you think I'm going home with you, you're crazy. Make me. If you try and drag me out, I'll call the welfare department on you.'

"Several twenty-one-year-old young men walked into the room, lounging against the wall and looking like some kind of bodyguards for Sandy. I didn't know what to do. Of course, I was furious, but I knew that no shouting match or physical fight would help.

"Then I asked myself. What worries me most? Drugs, alcohol, sex. None of that would be as likely to happen if there were an adult present. With that, I walked over and sat down on the couch. I tried to act cool. 'Would you bring me something cold?' I asked. 'It looks like I'm going to have my first New Year's Eve party with teenagers in twenty years.'

"They were dumbfounded. They all went to the kitchen. I could hear their voices. 'Geez, Sandy, your father's staying.' About one minute later, Sandy emerged to announce, 'Well, if you think you're going to stay and wreck the party, then I'm going home.' By the time we were halfway home, Sandy was laughing and saying, 'I can't believe you came, Dad.' "

John couldn't resist the chance to expound his theories of parenting.

"You're going to have more troubles with your daughter," he pronounced. "You can't let children talk to you like that."

I found out later that John's daughter came home from the same party at three the next morning. They had a shouting match and he grounded her indefinitely. She ran away two hours later and he has never seen her since. John has spent more then five thousand dollars trying to locate his daughter, without result.

Meanwhile, Sandy went on to graduate from high school, obtain a job that she likes as a buyer for a department store and become engaged. The paradox is that John still considers Bill a wimp and himself the better parent.

The major criterion of good parenting, or good anything, is results. Bill got his daughter home. She has entered adult life with every expectation of doing well. John lost his daughter. I don't care how "good" John sounded, or how flexible Bill had to be, Bill is the better parent because his discipline (going and getting) was effective.

Working With: Coworkers, Not Slaves

The best way to teach anyone a skill is to work alongside the person and show as you go. If the primary meaning of discipline is teaching, then working together with your child to complete a task is good discipline. Parents will do better if they focus more on the completion of the task than on straightening out the child's mind.

Household chores are the best areas for this type of discipline. Saturday morning seems to be the time most houses are cleaned. Each child has a room to clean, with written directions on how to clean that room. No TV or going out is allowed until the whole house is finished. If everyone is done by noon, then Mom or Dad takes the helpers out to their favorite fast food restaurant for lunch. If not done by noon, then Mom and Dad finish the job themselves, without the rewards of nagging *and* free lunch.

"Clean your room!" is an oft-heard parental admonition. A room that looks like a pig sty is the nemesis of many a parent. Much better than the parent nagging her child day after day would be to set a specific time to check. She goes to the child's room at that time. If it is clean, the child receives some token reward. If not, the parent and child clean the room together. No TV, or any other reward, until it is done.

Some parents, however, have objected to this technique, asking how the child will learn to clean on his own. Won't the child learn that Mom or Dad will help you if you don't do it? I have to laugh, because these are the very parents who are unsuccessful with the nagging method. Their child has learned that one gets a constant barrage of attention for a messy room.

With Mom or Dad helping, the child is learning two things, both very important. First, Mom's example teaches the child Mom means what she says. Even though Mom is not threatening or punitive about it, when she says to clean up the room, it gets cleaned up. Second, the example teaches the child *how* to clean up the room.

Distracting

Distracting becomes a key disciplinary technique when the child is doing something outrageous, like throwing a temper tantrum. One obvious purpose of the tantrum is to provoke a parental reaction. The good parent would like to avoid a confrontation and to avoid giving any attention to the tantrum, but often is stymied until the tantrum is over.

The child is asking for attention and probably needs it. But you can't give in to the unacceptable behavior. A good strategy is to distract the child, get her doing something worthwhile and then give her the attention for *that* activity.

Once the tantrum has started, however, it is very difficult to draw attention away from the tantrum. Rock-em, sock-em tantrums are not likely to be corrected either by explaining things or being reasonable. You need a two-step strategy.

As much as possible, you need to ignore the tantrum itself. If you are in a public place, you should leave. If the tantrum occurs at home, protect the child and any nearby items. Then let the screaming and hollering run its course.

In the meantime, make something available that may distract and interest the child. Keep some standby toys or activities saved up to be used as preventives for active youngsters with energy to burn. The purpose is to expend their high levels of energy in a variety of play activities. I call them "Active Itties." The more active and physical the alternate activity is, the more likely it is that the child will become distracted. This is not a reward for the temper tantrum. Rather it is an attempt to get him interested in something else so that you may again begin to pay attention to him, but for something worthwhile.

In fact, a good preventive goal would be to engage the child in an Active Itty regularly so that his high energy is used before it builds and explodes in a temper tantrum. Schedule one Active Itty for about one-half hour each day. Pick a time when you are already having trouble controlling the child. Write out your time and activity schedule a week in advance, with his advice. He will have something to look forward to each day. Here are some possibilities:

1) Stack, cut and color large boxes to make houses out of them. Add blankets to make a fort.

2) Buy some old clothes from a thrift shop or yard sale for "dress-up" play. They even can be colored and cut up.

3) Play indoor basketball. Use a soft, foam ball and a tin-can hoop.

4) Make homemade play dough (baker's clay) out of flour,

salt and water. Mix four cups of flour with one cup of salt; add one and one-half cups of water. Stir, then knead the mixture until thickened. After sculpting, the figures can be baked on a greased cookie sheet in the oven for about an hour. Store the dough in a sealed container in the refrigerator.

5) Anything in water can be fun: in the bathtub, at the sink or outdoors with the hose. A little preparation can make it possible. And remember to supervise your child at all times.

6) Paint some pictures on computer paper or scrap paper. Use finger paints if you are brave. Or add a generous amount of ordinary food color to a small dish of water. Spread out lots of old newspapers, preferably pages with lots of pictures. Let your children color the newspaper, using a pastry brush and the food-colored water. Inexpensive, watercolor, non-toxic paint sets can be purchased at a variety store for under two dollars.

7) Set a foam mattress on the floor for tumbling or gymnastics.

8) Put up a punching bag and flail away.

9) Form a band, using pots and pans for instruments. March around the house making "music."

10) Play a country-western or rock album and do some aerobic dancing. Or do an aerobic workout together.

Your children will soon let you know which activities work. If you're lucky, their favorites will also be yours.

Make Discipline a Game

A single parent friend of mine was dismayed one afternoon to hear a screech of brakes, followed by a car door opening and the sound of running footsteps. The front door opened and slammed shut as her nine-year-old son raced in. Then came the pounding on the door. Mother answered, to face a strange man, apparently a passing motorist.

"Your son gave me 'the finger' as I went by," he fumed. "When I slowed down, he called me an unrepeatable name." Mother had sufficient presence of mind to apologize and promise to correct her son.

When she confronted her son, he denied it. She did not argue, simply told him never to do that again. Then she took him outside.

"I have my watch here," she said. "I bet you can't run around the house in less than thirty seconds."

He took up her challenge. "I can too," he replied, and started to run around the house.

She recorded his time and paid him twenty-five cents. She now keeps a chart of his times, records them and pays him twenty-five cents every time he beats his best time.

She's a wise mother. She refused to get suckered into an attention-giving argument about what her son did and why it was wrong. She even avoided any time-consuming punishment. The last time something like this happened, she sent him to his room. He responded by destroying his stereo and breaking the window. She might have chosen to increase the punishment, but she decided she was getting nowhere with it. Instead, she took advantage of his high energy level and exuberance to distract him. Her method is working. Since they've started to race, there have been no more outrageous provocative incidents. It is better to give attention to racing around the house than to finger-flipping.

Discipline is not like medicine. It doesn't have to taste bad to be good for you. Good discipline can be fun and work very well. The crucial matter is the outcome— whether the parent gets the desired behavior, not whether the child suffers for the misdeeds. Here are a few more examples of good discipline games to inspire you.

Magic Word

As I said earlier, mealtime can become an occasion for arguing, complaining and just plain noise. When this occurs, one father initiates a family game to restore order. He utters a nonsense word, "Shazaam!" and all family members know they must instantly be silent. The meal progresses in total silence until the father says the second nonsense word, "Mustache." Each person who has maintained perfect silence during the interval receives a jelly bean. The silly game is more fun than a command to be quiet.

A nonsense word, a whistle, anything can be used to interrupt an out-of-control episode. Agree upon a funny word, like "Rumpelstiltskin," "Grandpa's outhouse." When the magic word is uttered, you must follow a previously agreed-upon routine. For example, Mom goes to the kitchen, Billy goes to the living room and everyone stays there for thirty seconds, long enough to lower the excitement level. Everyone who plays the game gets a peanut (or a penny or a raisin). Magic Word is more attractive than yelling "shut up." And it works better.

Quiet Chair

Four-year-old Susie is being mischievous again, teasing her baby brother. Dad asks her to leave her brother alone, but she simply waits until Dad's back is turned to start again. Dad catches her out of the corner of his eye and yells "Bonkers."

That is Susie's cue to play the Quiet Chair game, to turn to a special chair in the living room called the Good Girl chair. She must sit there and be quiet for about half a minute, until Dad gives the all-clear signal by saying "Pickle." If Susie remains quietly in her chair for the brief interlude between Bonkers and Pickle, she receives one piece of shredded wheat cereal covered with peanut butter, her favorite treat.

Susie plays Quiet Chair with the same enthusiasm she was teasing her brother. The game is good discipline because it works. It stops the teasing.

Mirror

This is a game, but perhaps not quite so much fun for the child as the other examples. In Mirror the parent reflects back to the child what the child has said or what the child appears to be feeling.

"I don't want to stay home. I'm going with you to the store," the child insists for the tenth time.

"I understand you want to go to the store," repeats the parent.

Instead of arguing, the parent simply restates what the child says, without giving in.

In another version, the parent copies facial expressions of the child. If the child cries, so does the parent. If the child looks angry, the parent makes an angry face too.

In still another version, the parent gets out the tape recorder, announcing:

"You've got some good points to make. I'd like to get them down on tape so that we can both listen to them later."

Be careful not to be sarcastic. This is easy to do with Mirror, to slip from mere mimicry into mocking and making fun of the child. It is better to think of it as a game of Copycat or Simon Says.

"I'm going to copy everything you do," says the parent.

The purpose is not to hurt or anger the child but to stop the continuing annoying behavior. Ideally, the child will become mildly frustrated at hearing his comments repeated and go on to do something else.

Reward Good Behavior

Like love, rewards can be unconditional or conditional. As I said earlier, unconditional rewards are given to the person just for being who he or she is. Conditional rewards depend on the occurrence of certain good behaviors. Sometimes called reinforcers, they are provided only when the child does what she is supposed to do.

Some parents argue that virtue is its own reward. The true merits of good behavior, they say, are spoiled when parents provide some tangible recognition or reward. Children ought to be good simply for the sake of being good.

That is a nice theory, but it is not the way behavior works. People stop doing certain things when those things are ignored or punished. They continue things that receive time and attention from others.

Parents who object to rewarding good behavior in their children are themselves just as susceptible to attentiveness from their friends as anyone else. They are enthusiastic when their listener smiles. They change the subject when he looks bored. Sometimes parents who are skeptical about rewards can be convinced to change their attitudes simply by looking at their own behaviors, noticing how they respond to reinforcement.

Another parental objection is that the reward is a bribe. "Must we bribe our children to be good?" The answer is that a reward is not a bribe. A bribe implies offering a reward to encourage illegal or immoral behavior. Good behavior is neither. In fact, good behavior is attractive and cries out to be noticed.

No one objects to wages for work or says that wages are merely a bribe to get a person to do something unpleasant but necessary. People work for wages. Generally speaking, the higher the wages, the more people will work. The major difference between wages and rewards is that wages are one's just due, whereas rewards can be freely given or withheld.

An excellent rule of thumb for parents is to make sure that more than half of the time and attention they give to their child is for desirable behavior. Some parents spend as much as ninety percent of their contact time correcting their child and criticizing misbehavior. To reverse this negative focus is not always easy. It requires considerable parental reflection on exactly what it is they would like their child to do.

Review problems together as parents. If you're a single parent, discuss the problems with a close friend. Figure out what to do next. Then spend the rest of the conversation taking inventory of your child's good points. In this way, you can remind each other about those good behaviors that may be neglected or overlooked. A strategy of paying attention to and building on good behaviors is preferable to one that simply tries to suppress the bad.

Ideally, you will target carefully certain desirable behaviors and provide specific rewards for the desirable behaviors you wish to encourage. How different this style is from the usual lecturing and nagging. Wise parents take the time and attention they might normally spend in scolding and apply it directly to a behavior they wish to encourage. Everyone needs attention. Desirable behavior, not undesirable, should get the payoff.

Charting Behavior

Charting is nothing more than a graphic way of formally rewarding behavior. Another name for charting might be behavioral bookkeeping. The chart is a written record of the date and the target behavior with a space left blank where it will be noted whether the child did the activity or not.

Charting works, just like it did for the wise mother in the finger-flipping example earlier. Any behavior that someone notices is likely to increase. Parents can keep daily charts on a dry bed, curfews, chores, television-watching time, dieting or almost any other behavior. Charts work best when they are kept in a public place, taped to the refrigerator or the bathroom wall. The chart itself, by providing attention, is a reward.

Charting is a very good way to implement the two basic rules, explained in this chapter and Chapter Three: (a) pay attention to the behavior wanted, and (b) discipline is learning, not just punishment. Most of us have been programmed to respond to misbehavior. Charting reminds us to identify carefully the good behavior we are seeking and to keep track of it when it occurs.

Charting is effective for all ages, from age three to senescence. As long as one can understand the meaning of a point or a sticker, receiving credit for each instance of "good" behavior is an excellent strategy for increasing that behavior.

We are all statisticians. Toddlers will brush their teeth, comb their hair and put away their clothes for stickers or smile faces. School-aged youngsters will work for grades and points. Athletes of all ages will perform mightily to record more rebounds, free throws, total yards, fumble recoveries, laps swum, miles run, spikes, goals or whatever the object of the event.

Adults work to achieve work rate or bonus rate, to amass points so they may earn premium gifts, to go to McDonald's and receive slips for free french fries. What is being counted may differ by age, but the method of charting is valid for every age.

Parents could ask their children for charting help in getting rid of their own bad habits. One child, at her mother's request, recorded the number of cigarettes Mom smoked each day. As Mom saw the lower numbers appear on the refrigerator each night, she gained motivation to quit for good. Another child kept note of his father's weekly weight. The weight was recorded, and every time Dad was under 160 pounds, the child received fifty cents. Needless to say, the child was rooting for his Dad to stay trim.

Token Economies

The target behavior is made explicit in charting. In token economies, the reward is also made explicit. Charting and token economies are often used together.

The token is the wage or payoff to be received for specified desirable behaviors. Tokens, like money, are a medium of exchange. They have a certain prestige value in themselves and they can be used for other desired items.

Most people recognize that Green Stamps are a token economy. When the adult is good, that is, when he buys lots of merchandise at the right stores, he gets to put lots of tokens (stamps) in his book. When he has enough stamps, he is rewarded by being able to purchase items at the premium redemption stores or through the catalog. A whole industry is testament to the fact that token economies work. What works for adults will work for children too.

Some commonly used tokens are gold stars, ribbons, stickers, pennies, poker chips, points, smile faces or pluses. The tokens can be awarded directly or entered on a chart.

In its simplest form, parents award the token when the specified behavior is performed. For example, John gets a point for being downstairs and ready for breakfast by seven o'clock. Sharon gets a small ribbon for completing her half-hour piano practice. Alan gets a poker chip for setting the dinner table before five-thirty.

The children can turn in their tokens for a choice of rewards. These rewards can be toys, privileges or anything else. For example, each token may be redeemable for a small amount of money. Two tokens may buy an extra hour of television. A shopping trip with lunch may cost twenty-five tokens. A new bike may have a price tag of one hundred fifty tokens.

One mother simply bought about fifteen small toys. She tagged each one with a price in tokens; her child could go shopping whenever he had enough tokens. Both the token and the shopping were the rewards for being good.

A token economy works best when there are a few inexpensive items that can be purchased almost immediately and a few high-priced ones that require some saving. The child then has the possibility of either immediate gratification or saving for a highly valued item.

Endless variation is possible. Tokens can be given the broadest interpretation. One mother lets her child put his hand in the treasure jar whenever he makes his bed. In the jar are many slips of paper with small silly rewards: "Good for one hug." "Collect one story." "Worth two cents." The surprise is half the fun, not to mention the fun Mom and Dad have making the slips.

Another mother puts a smile face on a chart every time she hears her child say something kind to someone else. Two smile faces merit a reach in the peanut jar and all the roasted peanuts the child can hold in her hand. Yet another mother gives a raisin every time her shy child talks and socializes in a communicative way.

The advantage of token economies is that they are positive and require a specific observable target. When they fail, it is usually for one of three reasons. The first is that parents choose a reward that is not really perceived as one by the child. Parents need to know, understand and use what their child values.

The second reason for failure is that parents forget to give the tokens or delay in providing the reward. Remember that rewards must be immediate and certain. The token must be awarded as soon as possible after the good behavior, and the child must be allowed to spend the tokens whenever wished. That is part of the agreement.

The third reason for failure is that some parents decide to take away tokens as a punishment for bad behavior. The fact that the child values the tokens is evidence that the system is working well. When the child does something naughty, the parent, seeking to make the child realize how naughty she has been, subtracts some of the valued tokens the child has earned for good behavior. Once earned, a token should be enjoyed and spent. It is not subject to recall. If punishment is desired or required, parents should find some other penalty (re-read the beginning of this chapter for ideas). Subtracting tokens will cause the system to fail.

Behavior Contracting

Carrie, a fifteen-year-old high school sophomore, had gone from being tardy to being truant because her best friend liked to skip school. Then she ran away because she claimed her parents were "always nagging me or grounding me forever for something and won't get off my back." The parents were ready to throw up their hands in defeat and were talking about putting Carrie in a foster home placement.

Fortunately, Carrie and her parents were able to talk out their conflict. When Carrie was asked what she wanted most, she said: "Freedom to spend time with my friends." When asked what she most resented she replied: "Being grounded indefinitely."

Carrie's parents, when asked to specify what they felt was the most important issue or problem, identified Carrie's school attendance. Both Carrie and her parents, however, were so hurt and angry, and their feelings were so strong, that it appeared doubtful the discussion could lead to any behavioral change. A behavioral contract helped to defuse the situation and turned out to be a remedy by which both sides gained.

Much negotiation was required. At times, the conversation sounded like a labor-management dispute. In the end, both sides compromised. Carrie and her parents agreed to a behavior contract in writing.

Carrie wrote: "I agree to attend all my classes and to be there on time. I also agree that for every class I miss, I must perform one hour of housework under my mother's supervision before I can go out again. I further agree to be home by nine o'clock on school nights and ten o'clock on weekends." Carrie signed it.

Her parents wrote: "We agree not to nag Carrie about her school attendance. Instead, we will check with the school counselor each day to determine if she has attended all her classes. For every class she has attended and arrived at on time, we will give Carrie one freedom point. Each freedom point is worth ten minutes beyond curfew or late time. We agree that Carrie can save these points and use them to stay out past her curfew when she wishes. We further agree not to ground Carrie indefinitely but allow her to work off her penalty for truancy at the rate of one hour of housework for each school class missed. She must stay home until her penalty is completed, but then she will be free to go out again." Her parents signed their part.

Although the agreement sounds simple, it took a long time to achieve. The first obstacle was the strong negative feelings on both sides. Concentrating on the behaviors rather than the emotions helped to sidestep some of the emotions. A second obstacle involved the parents' reluctance to accept their daughter as an equal in the negotiating process. Equality represented a big change for them, since they were used to giving help or orders to a dependent child. Now they were dealing with someone who had demonstrated that she could, in fact, defy and defeat them by running away. The parents did not like this circumstance, but they felt it was still better than losing their daughter to a foster home.

From then on, the obstacles were more situational. Carrie did not want to agree to attend all her classes, nor did she feel she should have any curfew. She felt she was an adult already and should be able to set her own hours. On the other hand, her father and mother were uneasy about giving up the right to ground Carrie indefinitely. Her father especially was uneasy about letting Carrie save up enough points to stay out very late, perhaps even all night. He finally agreed when Carrie's mother pointed out that even this would be an improvement, since Carrie had already run away twice. If Carrie attended her classes and only stayed out late when she had earned it, her mother felt that would be considerable progress. Her father thought about it for a time and agreed.

Behavior contracts can be negotiated at any age, provided the child is old enough to understand the nature of a contract. Behavior contracts are commonly used less formally and in less dramatic situations. One parent says: "If you keep your room clean for a week, I'll take you out to lunch on Saturday." In this case, the terms are rather general and the contract is oral. If it works, fine. If not, parents may need to get more specific about the conditions, putting the goal and reward in writing. Putting the conditions on paper leaves less room for vagueness and arbitrary interpretation.

Behavior contracts can help with teenagers, especially when strong emotions have led to an impasse. By concentrating on parent-child actions rather than on the anger, both parties can be more objective. A behavior contract offers parents and children a chance to calm down and treat the matter realistically.

The major roadblock is that parents must give up some power. Actually, what they give up is only the illusion of power, since the child already may be successfully defying the parents with such behavior as drug abuse, truancy and running away from home.

A good behavior contract, one that is likely to work, will usually have four qualities. It will be (a) mutual and (b) detailed, (c) it will include both a reward and a penalty and (d) it will be honored.

Mutual means that it will probably involve some compromises and that all parties will have an opportunity for input and disagreement. More to the point, the child must be heard fairly, and his suggestions and objections considered. Otherwise, the contract is not an agreement but one more parental mandate.

Detailed means that all the behaviors to be expected of both parents and child must be spelled out clearly and in writing. The penalties for noncompliance must also be written out in specific language. Usually, this guarantee provides welcome relief for the child from what she perceives as parental overreaction to misbehavior or parental moods. The child knows exactly what will be imposed as a penalty for misbehavior. For example, Carrie knows she will not be grounded forever but will have a specified number of hours of hard work if she cuts classes.

Both a *reward* and a *penalty* for specific behavior should be provided. In Carrie's case, if she attended her classes, her parents were willing to let her stay out later at night.

Finally, a good contract must be *honored*. A deal is a deal. When parents get the desired behavior, they sometimes become reluctant to let their child do whatever it is they had originally agreed upon in the contract. If the child fails to honor the terms of the contract, then either the terms need renegotiation or perhaps her parents need to develop a new plan of discipline.

Some parents may still object that a behavior contract gives in to the child. Nothing could be more incorrect. If giving the child commands is not working, then a behavior contract may be another way to achieve parental objectives. Parents must keep clearly in mind the goal: to receive and encourage the desired behavior.

Sample Charts and Contracts

Charting and contracting are not difficult. They just require that parents are consistent in writing things down and keeping track. That consistency forces the parents and child to be very practical and specific. Here are a few examples applying charting and contracting to some universal child-rearing issues.

Bedwetting

The first advantage in using the techniques with this problem is that the parents are immediately required to change the target from bedwetting to its opposite—staying dry.

Contract: Mark agrees to take care of himself if he wets the bed. He will strip his bed and place his pajamas and sheets by the washer. His parents agree to say nothing.

If Mark stays dry, he will receive one smile face on his success chart. For every three smile faces, he will receive a small gift. If he wets, his parents will simply mark an X on the chart.

Stay-Dry Nights Success				
	Week One	**Week Two**	**Week Three**	**Week Four**
Sunday				
Monday				
Tuesday				
Wednesday				
Thursday				
Friday				
Saturday				

Cleaning House

Beginning housekeepers at motels are often given a three-month training period. Too often, young children are simply ordered to clean a room. Parents need to teach children how to clean.

Children need very specific instructions. A parent should personally go through the steps in cleaning a room, specifying each step along with the materials to be used. Each child should have a cleaning caddy stocked with supplies.

The parent should design an instruction list for each room that a child is expected to clean. The child has a copy of the list and checks off each step as it is completed. When the room is finished, the parent goes through the same list, checks the items that have been satisfactorily completed and returns the list for the child to finish the incomplete steps.

Here are a sample contract and some simple instructions on how to clean a room properly.

Contract: The children agree to clean house on Saturday mornings, beginning at nine. No one may leave the house or watch TV until all rooms are satisfactorily cleaned. Mom or Dad will check each room at eleven. Each child will receive two dollars for each room satisfactorily cleaned. All children who have cleaned at least one room will go out to lunch with Mom or Dad at noon.

Housecleaning		
Date:	**Cleaner**	**Score (+ or -)**
Living room	Sandy	
Dining room	Bob	
TV room	Pete	
Bathroom	Sue	

How to Clean the TV Room

1) Pick up and put away items. Please sort the preschool toys and put them in the toy storage. Do not dump them all together and hide them somewhere. Return all VCR tapes to the storage cabinet by title in alphabetical order.

2) Empty the wastebasket.

3) With the vacuum and dust brush, dust the windowsills

and frames, the painted bookcase, the top of the TV and the shelf of the TV cart.

4) Clean the TV screen with glass cleaner and paper towels.

5) Clean the corner table with a clean, damp sponge.

6) Vacuum the sofa cushions, all sides, using the furniture attachment with the vacuum.

7) Vacuum the floor.

8) With all-purpose cleaner and a clean rag, spot clean the painted doors, window frames and bookcases.

9) Take the dirty rags to the laundry room for washing. Refill the cleaning caddy with clean rags and fresh supplies.

How to Clean the Bathroom

1) Pick up and put away everything that doesn't belong. Remove everything from the floor.

2) Flush the toilet. Measure one-half cup bleach and pour into the toilet.

3) Using all-purpose cleaner and a rag, wash the sink, the counter, the toilet tank, the toilet seat and the outside of the toilet. Spot clean the light switch, the door frame and the door as needed.

4) Clean the drinking cups with detergent and rinse. Or take the cups to the kitchen and replace them with clean ones.

5) With window cleaner and a paper towel, clean the mirror and faucets, the sink and the tub faucets.

6) Now scrub the toilet with the toilet brush. Rinse the brush in the sink and leave the bleach in the toilet.

7) Clean the tub with all-purpose cleanser and a rag.

8) Vacuum the floor with the floor brush. Fill a bucket

one-third full with plain water, then add one-quarter cup of all-purpose cleaner. Clean the floor with a large sponge.

9) While waiting for the floor to dry, vacuum the hall outside the bathroom. Empty the wastebasket. Take the throw rug outdoors and shake it vigorously.

10) When the floor is dry, put the throw rug and scale back in the bathroom. Take the dirty rags to the laundry room for washing. Replace the cleaning supplies in the caddy.

Clean Your Room!

Trying to get a child to pick up his or her room probably provokes more nagging than any other parent-child issue. Many parents are frustrated. Some give up. Here is a simple way to contract and chart for a clean room.

Contract: Mike agrees to clean his room and put it in order each day. Mom or Dad will inspect the room at 7 p.m. each day. For every item on the chart that has been completed, the parent will award Mike one bonus point. For every item still to be done, the parent will write in a zero. There will be no scolding or nagging. The parents and Mike will then finish cleaning the room together. For every ten points, Mike may pull a slip out of the love jar. On each slip the parent will have written an attractive surprise. Examples might include a hug, breakfast in bed, a music tape, fifty cents, Dad will do your chores or even something humorous like Dad promising to stand on his head for ten seconds.

A Clean Room											
Date	1	2	3	4	5	6	7	8	9	10	etc.
Bed made											
Floor clean											
Under bed clean											
Dirty clothes in hamper											
Clean clothes in drawer											
Dresser top clean											
Daily points											

Bad Mouth/Happy Mouth

Perhaps because of the verbal license on television, young teens today like to "smart off" to their parents or use profanity. This can trigger Mom or Dad's temper. As with the previous contracts and charts, the first step is to invert the target—and select "Happy Mouth" rather than "Bad Mouth" for parental discipline and attention. Note that the specific "dirty" words are written right into the contract.

Contract: Lisa agrees not to raise her voice in anger and not to say "f___," "bitch" or "screw." She will receive one smile face for each half day she is free of "smart" or "dirty" language. One smile face equals one point. Mom recognizes that it is hard for Lisa to control her mouth, so that is Mom's way of saying thank you. If Lisa should slip, Mom will not react but will simply give Lisa an X for that half day.

Happy Mouth			
	Before 3 p.m.	After 3 p.m.	Daily points
Sunday			
Monday			
Tuesday			
Wednesday			
Thursday			
Friday			
Saturday			

Smile faces may be used as follows:

> Car time: fifteen minutes = one point.
>
> Late time: fifteen minutes = one point (Lisa must tell Mom in advance. Eleven-thirty is the latest).
>
> Skip supper: one point.
>
> Money: ten cents = one point.
>
> Chauffeur: four-mile trip = two points.
>
> Overnight: Stay over at friend's = ten points.
>
> Have a friend over = five points.

CHAPTER FIVE

One of These Days We've Got to Get Organized: Scheduling

I often ask parents to name their major child-rearing problems. Teaching children responsibility is near the top of every parent's list. One of the best ways to do this is to run a reasonably orderly household, where the rules are clear and parents follow through to see that chores are done and children get home on time.

House Rules

Most smooth-running households have rules. House rules are a way of structuring the environment to make harmonious family living possible, even probable. House rules are for the good of all the members and are not primarily intended to teach responsibility and obedience. Nevertheless, they do provide valuable lessons in living with other people. Making and enforcing house rules constitute a large part of discipline. An appropriate set of house rules allows the positive parent to act rather then merely react. They help parents to program for good behavior in advance while anticipating and precontrolling some of the bad.

Each family expects certain things of its children, but they differ on which things. House rules vary. Probably all families agree that stealing, lying and hitting are unacceptable. Some families emphasize completing assigned jobs. Others demand that rooms and possessions always be neat and orderly. For other families good manners and punctuality are of primary importance.

Household Chores

The child who is required to do household chores benefits in ways that go far beyond learning some basic cooking and cleaning skills. Children, like persons of any age, need to be needed. With a work assignment, the adult says to the child: "Not only do I need you, but I value you. I trust you. I have confidence that you can do this job or I would not give it to you." The child clearly is important.

Assigning chores says not only that the children are important as individuals, but that they belong and contribute to the family. Children are not pampered pets to be indulged and waited upon but contributing members of a worthwhile enterprise. Children who have something to contribute learn to feel good about themselves. People who feel good about themselves have a greater capacity to love others.

Finally, assigning chores presents housework as a collection of jobs to be shared by various members of the family rather than a task to be completed by just one member. The children learn that this is the family's house and everyone contributes to its care. The child who is not given household chores is shortchanged.

The type of chore assigned depends upon the age. Four- or five-year-old children can help set the table and straighten a room. By six or seven, a child can wash the dishes and clean a room acceptably with training. The younger the child, the more specific the instructions must be and the longer the parent must work along with the child.

Elementary-school-aged children should be able to help with almost any routine household task. Middle-school-aged children may be the most industrious. They cannot yet obtain a regular paying job outside the home and are often willing workers. By high school, interests outside the family are increasing, and more motivation may be necessary to induce older children to complete their chores.

In some families the help provided by the children may be essential, for example when there is only one parent, when both Mom and Dad have jobs or volunteer work outside the home or when there is an infant in the family. In a sense, these children may be lucky. They can grow through the important jobs they do and the rules they follow.

In other cases, Mom or Dad may have the time and desire to do the housework alone. "Why bother with the children?" may be the thought. It does take longer to teach and supervise a child than to do it alone. If the parent does accept help from the child, it may be received as only token assistance and the job may be re-done when the child is finished.

Tokenism has the opposite effect on a child than doing important chores. Tokenism tells the child: "You can't do very much, and what you do isn't done well enough. I have to do most of the work." Such a parent needs to grow by learning to accept help. Not doing so deprives the child of the sense of competence and belonging that can be gained by doing chores.

The Blake family has two parents, one grandfather and five children, ages four to nineteen. They have evolved three kinds of chores to divide the work. The daily jobs are in the first group: helping with breakfast, cleaning up after dinner, washing the dinner dishes, setting and clearing the table and cooking Saturday night dinner. These jobs rotate every month. They involve no pay but are performed because each child is a contributing member of the family.

When the job assignment conflicts with sports practice or a birthday party, the child must trade with another family member. If the child fails to do the job or comes in late, no parental pressure is required. The whole family suffers and the whole family lets the offender know. Dinner for all may be delayed an hour. That happens very rarely at the Blake house.

A second set of jobs is housecleaning every Saturday morning. Mom or Dad supervises while each member does the appointed task. Refer to the charts in Chapter Four for help with assigning the housecleaning jobs. The children are paid for these jobs. They may subcontract their assignment to another family member if they wish, but the task must be completed by noon on Saturday.

Finally, there are special jobs that come up occasionally such as washing windows or painting walls. The Blakes pay a minimum wage for these jobs and find a family member who needs the money. Usually that will be a child age nine to fourteen, too young to work at a regular job but old enough to know the joy and power of money.

The Blakes admit that for the first few weeks in the system the children's efforts were almost more trouble than they were worth. They had to be taught, reminded and checked on. But following detailed job descriptions, similar to the ones in Chapter Four, aided the children in their "training period."

When the older Blake girl comes home from college, she acts as a volunteer substitute for any of the younger ones who cannot do their jobs for some reason. When Mom was sick, the Blakes took turns cooking complete dinners, something they had learned on Saturday nights. When elderly neighbors need housework done, they hire one of the Blake children. The second-grader summed up how well the system is working during show-and-tell time at school. When asked what he did at home, he said quite seriously, "I practically run the family."

Not every family has five children, but there is much wisdom in the Blake approach that can be adapted for the smaller family. Chore schedules might be less elaborate. In any household, children can gain skills, self-esteem and confidence from jobs well done.

In summary, here are basic rules to follow to help your children become capable household helpers:

1) Select tasks within the child's capability. Assign only the number of jobs you can teach and supervise. And assign real jobs. Some mothers cook a five-course meal while Susie stirs the gravy. They then exclaim, "Susie cooked dinner." Such false enthusiasm is demeaning and fools no one, certainly not the child. Give Susie jobs she can really *do* and compliment her for genuine competency.

2) Take the time to teach your child the right way. Many parents fail on this point because teaching a task demands much of the parent.

    Figure out step-by-step how you want your child to clean the bathroom. Write down each step, using a checklist. Follow the sample checklists provided in Chapter Four. Most children like to follow a checklist and enjoy the satisfaction of reaching the end. If you do not specify each job, be assured it will not be done.

    Work along with the child a couple of times. Demonstrate the task and give the child a chance to do it.

3) Specify a time to do chores. If no time is set, the child can always promise to do them later.

4) Do not expect your child to be enthusiastic about developing his capabilities and self-esteem through chores. Work is work. Most likely the child will gripe; the object of the gripes will be you. As a good disciplinarian allow the child to express the gripes, but see that the chore is done.

5) Decide in advance whether the children get paid, whether they get some other reward or whether they are expected to do this job as their contribution to the family. Children like to know what to expect.

6) Once your children can do the job adequately, let them alone when they work. Don't hover around, criticize or give advice. When they have finished, check their work. Point out any oversights, and above all, notice and appreciate a job well done.

On Time

Being on time for dinner, getting up on time and going to bed on time are important rules in many families. In families as well as businesses, punctuality is not only a virtue but a necessity.

For preschoolers, parents can enforce punctuality by actually going and getting the child when it's time for dinner or bed or time to wake up. Once a child is able to roam a little farther from home, however, parents must find ways to motivate on-time behavior, either through consequences or rewards.

Being on Time for Dinner

Many a mother has lost her composure when family members have shown up late for dinner. One child complains, "We never eat at five-thirty like everyone else." But Dad never gets home until six o'clock. And no one knows when older brother is likely to arrive. Mother fixes a nutritious and delicious dinner, but no one is there at the right time to eat it.

It is very appropriate to set a specific mealtime and appropriate consequences for late arrivals. Being late for dinner can have such obvious consequences that scolding, nagging or any form of punishment would seem irrelevant. The logical consequence would be to require the latecomer to fix his or her own dinner and clean up afterward. Another logical consequence would be the rule that anyone late for dinner must do all the dishes. The job must be done anyway and who better to do it than the person who inconvenienced the rest of the family.

Waking up on Time

One parent complained: "In the winter he's late for school. In the summer he's late for everything. My seven-year-old is the worst procrastinator. I get after him to get up, make his bed, brush his teeth, get dressed. The more I get after him, the worse he gets. Eventually I get frustrated and start yelling. Half the time he misses the school bus and we have to drive him to school. How do we get him up and off to school on time?"

Procrastination is a common enough problem, not only among children but adults as well. The above parent is probably making it worse by nagging the child all the time. What she needs is a plan that moves her son along without giving him too much attention for delaying tactics.

One possible approach would be for her to back off and let her son suffer the consequences of his foot-dragging, such as missing school when he misses the bus. Allowing him to miss school more than once or twice, however, is not wise.

Here is a better plan, which should minimize the attention she gives to pokiness. This plan will take some of her time. From what she describes, however, it will take less time than she now loses with the ineffective nagging.

She should break up the task of getting up and ready into smaller units, then follow through on each one, not with her words but her actions. This plan should move her son along with a minimum of rewarding attention. Here is a sample schedule:

Wake-up Schedule		
Task	**Deadline**	**Points**
Get up	6:30 a.m.	
Dress	6:35 a.m.	
Make bed	6:50 a.m.	
Eat breakfast	6:55 a.m.	
Finished with breakfast	7:10 a.m.	
Brush teeth	7:15 a.m.	
Get school books together	7:20 a.m.	
At bus stop	7:30 a.m.	

Mom can set the oven timer for each deadline and check on her son. If he has not completed the task, she should do it for or with him and say nothing. If he has completed the task, she gives him a point on the chart.

In the preceding plan he can earn as many as eight points each morning. Mom and he can arrange several small treats or activities which can be purchased with the points earned.

This plan has several advantages. First of all, trying to finish before the buzzer rings can become a challenging game. Kids also like to see points accumulate.

Furthermore, now Mom's attention is provided primarily for achievements. Before, most of her attention was given for delaying.

Finally, this plan works. Since she will be moving her son along at each step, he is more likely to be ready for the bus. It is not bad to help him. Rather, he will learn that Mom means what she says about being ready. He also will learn from her example.

Going to Bed on Time

A bedtime may or may not be required. Like hunger,
fatigue will eventually catch up with any child and send her
off to sleep. Parents need not insist on a bedtime for their
child's sake. Nature will usually take care of that. The
parents, however, may need to insist on a bedtime for *their*
sake.

Parents deserve some time for each other and
themselves. Most parents would like at least one hour of
freedom from all their children's homework, requests and
love before they themselves go to bed. Hence, it is
reasonable to set a bedtime for the children about an hour
before that of the parents. Younger children can be
expected to go to bed earlier still. It is debatable whether
teenagers can be expected to go to bed at all! But up to
about age twelve, a bedtime of nine o'clock or nine-thirty
seems reasonable.

The Bertrams insist that their eight- and ten-year-old
children be in bed by nine o'clock. They allow reading in
bed, listening to the radio and whispering to each other.
They do not allow homework, games or horseplay in bed.
The Bertrams have a good idea, especially since it may
encourage that much-neglected activity—reading.

Parenting Made Simpler

Carrying out the rules is not always easy, but the basic
rules of good discipline are simple enough. In Chapters
One through Five, I have suggested a precondition, two
elementary rules and ways to enact these rules.

Coping with your own stress is the precondition. If you,
the parent, are not in good health and doing well, then good
discipline may be impossible. Be gentle with yourself. Your
health and welfare are very important to your child.

The two rules are almost elementary. First, try to give
attention to good behavior and as little as possible to the

bad. Second, there are more and better ways to change behavior than through threats and punishment.

The ways to enact the rules are through discipline rather than punishment, positive reinforcement, charting and behavior contracting, and organization.

In Chapter Six, I answer common and difficult parenting questions directly. I focus on finding a way to obtain the desired outcome.

Thirty-Eight Questions Parents Ask

Some of the common parenting questions have already been addressed in preceding chapters: questions about homework, responsibility and getting rid of bad attitudes. Other common questions and answers to help you deal with the behavior follow.

Good parents ask hard questions. While the questions may be hard, the strategy remains the same. Apply the two principles. As much as possible, give attention only to behavior that you want to encourage. And broaden your discipline methods to include many more strategies than mere punishment.

1. Allowances: Should every child receive an allowance?

I am thinking of starting my oldest child, a first-grader, on an allowance. Could you give me some ideas about managing children's allowances?

I think allowances for children are a good idea. We live in a society where most transactions involve money. Helping a child to learn money management is part of parenting.

Allowances should start by age seven or eight. Before this time an allowance is a token. The child knows money is good to have and may wish to imitate friends or older brothers and sisters, but she has little sense of money value or use. The child will be equally satisfied with a nickel or a quarter.

Around eight the child begins to develop a sense of ownership—of acquiring, collecting and perhaps hoarding goods. According to research on child development, eight-year-olds are money-mad.

Rather than viewing such behavior as selfish and undesirable, parents should recognize that the child is in a new stage of growth. The child is trying to sort out the concepts of mine and yours, and what ownership means. An allowance can help him acquire this understanding.

An allowance is not a salary. It is a sign of unconditional parental love. It is the child's weekly share in the family wealth. He is entitled to it just because he *is*—no matter how lazy he is, no matter how badly he behaves.

When a child, young or old, cannot get by on the allowance, she has the same option as the rest of us—to work. I think children should do some daily chores simply because they are part of the household. On the other hand, if they do a special job which you would pay an outsider to do, then it is appropriate to pay them. I put window-washing and hand-polishing furniture in this category. For such jobs they deserve a salary. This, however, is not an allowance.

Do not withhold the allowance as a punishment. If you do, you make the allowance a reward or pay for being good. In order to learn responsibility, the child must be able to count on the allowance.

The allowance can be used, however, to curtail waste. Suppose your child loses or wastes too much paper, paste or crayons. You might make the allowance large enough to cover these items and have the child buy his own. Another plan, easier for eight-to-ten-year-olds, would be to supply a reasonable amount of school supplies each month. When the child runs out before the next month's supply, he must supplement it from his allowance.

An allowance is not an expense account. Let the child have as much choice as possible in spending the money. Don't pressure him. Specify the weekly sum. If there are some necessities which must be purchased out of that sum, specify those too. But remember, without freedom of choice the child will learn little about budgeting and spending money.

If any purchases are forbidden, those rules, too, should be specified when the allowance begins. If you want to set limits on candy, soft drinks, war comics or toy guns, set them in advance.

The number of items which the child must finance and the amount of the allowance should both increase over the years. From third to eighth grade, I recommend a range from twenty-five cents to two dollars per week, increasing every year or two.

By high school a child can handle all her expenses except room, board and medical care. Personally I can't imagine buying clothes for my teens. I simply wouldn't have the courage. For this I suggest an allowance of twenty-five to fifty dollars per month.

The advantages of the allowance system are many. An allowance helps a child learn about ownership. It spares parents from the temptation to be arbitrary, rewarding children with money when life seems to flow smoothly and refusing their requests when things go badly. It frees parents from the hassle of making a decision over every trivial request: "May I have this? May I have that?"

Through an allowance the child gains some independence from parents and some responsibility for meeting personal needs. It helps the child to grow.

2. Big Mouth: How do you silence rudeness and defiance?

We have a fifteen-year-old daughter who is setting the whole family on edge with her mouth. She says whatever she thinks or feels, however rude or critical, to anyone in the family. We have tried to silence her by isolating her, but without success. What alternatives do we have?

Most crises that affect teenagers are not caused by the family, but the family bears the brunt of the problem. Teens get upset over schoolwork, teachers, differences with girlfriends or boyfriends, performance in music or sports and a host of other situations.

In most situations they cannot mouth off but must keep their anger or frustration inside. Once they get home, the family gets all the pent-up frustration in the form of meanness, criticism or yelling.

Parents distressed by rude remarks are often doubly upset because they feel that the criticism is against them. Somehow they are at fault. Most likely the teen's frustration has little or nothing to do with the parents' behavior. Home is simply the one place the teen feels free to let off steam.

Telling an angry teen to be quiet is usually futile as you have discovered. Your suggestion of isolation for brief periods is a good one. The teen cannot yell or be rude if there is no one there to attack verbally.

Send your daughter to her room for a brief period of time, just long enough to break the verbal tirade. And use this tactic only when you need some relief.

Ideally, to change her behavior, you would like to pay little or no attention to the rude, mean remarks and plenty of attention to any cooperative, normal conversation. This is not easy. How can you ignore meanness and yelling? Suppose she never talks normally. What then?

To pinpoint the trouble spots, pick the time of day you find most difficult. Perhaps it is around the dinner hour. Everyone is tired and hungry and your daughter begins her attack. For a few days observe just how much discord occurs. Make a chart, divide the hours into fifteen-minute periods and keep score. Every period free of mouthing off gets a plus; every period when mouthing does occur gets a minus.

Charting helps locate the worst periods, but it also makes you aware of the good moments.

Now try to increase the trouble-free times. Perhaps you will find that when your daughter helps out with dinner, she works more and mouths off less. A regular task—making salads, setting the table, doing the dishes—might stop the rude mouth temporarily and channel her pent-up frustration into positive behavior.

Whenever you find she is acting cooperatively, notice it. A compliment, a hug, an offer to help her with some project, are positive responses to good behavior. Be sure to give some positive reasons every time she is pleasant around the family. By focusing on the positive, you give your daughter more incentive to be civil and you force yourself to notice the good moments rather than dwell on the unpleasant ones.

Remember adolescents go through a tumultuous period. They find many ways to release their emotions. Yelling and rudeness, while unpleasant for the family, are fairly harmless outlets. These actions are likely to pass as your daughter is more comfortable with herself and as you reinforce her positive behavior with your attention.

3. Blaming Others: What can you do to get a child to admit he's wrong?

What can you do to get a child to admit a wrong? My twelve-year-old son always blames another. He never acknowledges his actions.

Your son, like most human beings of all ages, would like to get off the hook. How many times have you heard an accident explained with the excuse, "The car skidded," instead of, "I was driving too fast." Or a broken dinner plate is explained, "It fell," rather than "I carelessly knocked it off the table."

Comedian Flip Wilson entertained us all by projecting the blame onto forces from the other world. Every time his character misbehaved, he would dodge culpability with a grin and announce, "The devil made me do it."

How quick we are to sidestep responsibility. The tendency to blame the other guy is a normal defensive reaction, designed to protect our egos. Not only is blaming normal, but it is still more common in children, whose understanding of other people's feelings is less developed than an adult's understanding.

What is it you want of your son, self-blame? That is a lot to expect of a twelve-year-old. Even our legal system does not require that we incriminate ourselves. Further, self-blame may have the opposite effect from what you intend. Your son may accept the fact that he is a bad boy and decide to behave like one.

You do want your son to avoid blaming others. Blaming others, however, has its own consequences and will generally evoke its own discipline. The others who get blamed will have their own defensive reactions and will try to "straighten out" the story.

Most likely you want your son to learn from his mistakes and to behave better in the future. Good. Focus on this. There is no evidence that verbal acceptance of responsibility in young children results in their behaving better. The problem is that many of us parents spend long verbal monologues pinning the blame on our child, requiring that he admit he is wrong. The child learns to defend himself with increasing cleverness. We end up spending entirely too much attention on bad behavior, behavior that does not deserve so much time, behavior that needs to be eliminated rather than argued about.

Realize that your child is programmed to avoid punishment. His tendency to point in the other direction when parents or teachers are searching for the culprit is natural and not surprising.

You as a parent should assign responsibility as you see it. Be brief and direct, and follow your declaration with the consequence.

"The car may have skidded, but you were driving too fast for conditions. From now on, you must pay for your own auto insurance."

No argument. Do not fuss about whose fault it is. Move right to the outcome.

"You dropped the plate. Now clean it up."

"You did it, not the devil. In any case, it's you who must come home earlier from now on."

Finally, you will teach best by setting an example of responsible behavior. Apologize for losing your temper. Accept responsibility for your overeating and extra weight. If you as a parent can comfortably accept responsibility for your mistakes, your children will eventually follow the same mature path.

4. Bullies: How do I protect my child from bullies?

My ten-year-old son is constantly picked on by his classmates and even by younger children. The other children call him names like "stupid" and "weirdo." They also push him around and play mean jokes on him, like squashing his lunch bag. My husband and I are brokenhearted. He is our only child. We have talked to the school and complained to other parents but with no results. The abuse goes on. Please give us some suggestions about how to stop this before our son is destroyed. Shall we move?

I can understand your worry. It is hard to stand by and watch your son abused. You have tried to stop it without success. Now what can you do?

First, I would stop complaining to the other children's parents and the school. The complaining might be appropriate if only one or two bullies were involved. The harassing seems to follow a larger pattern. Continued complaining on your part may single your son out for special adult protection which in turn may lead to further teasing by his peers. If the adults try to forbid it, the teasing may become more hidden and subtle.

At the same time, do not try to isolate your son from his classmates. As an only child, he needs the opportunity to learn social skills for getting along with persons his own age.

Finally, do not move, at least not yet. You may be able to help your son reverse this pattern.

The best approach would be to try to find out what he does that elicits the abuse. When a child is picked on by most of his peers, it is wise to examine what the child does to invite the attacks. Often there is a victim psychology at work. Chronic victims behave in a way that draws fire. To say that the victim often evokes his own abuse is not to say that the victim is to blame. Bullying is always reprehensible. The most important action for you, however, is not to yell at bullies but to stop the abusive behavior. The best way to do that is to help your son change his behavior. He, not you, must learn how to avoid the meanness.

Let's look at an example.

A six-year-old came home beaten up.

"It's those big kids down the block," he cried.

Since this was the child's third such experience, his father decided to follow him on his next excursion. Riding his shiny new bike, the child proceeded down past the big kids and began to chant, "Nyah, nyah, see what I've got." Needless to say, the big kids began to chase him.

The father could have intervened by stopping the big kids and telling them to let his son alone. He felt it was much more important, however, to teach his son a few obvious alternative behaviors: Either stay away from big kids by going the other way or don't bring your new bike. And certainly don't say, "Nyah, nyah...."

Your son's behavior probably follows one of two common patterns. Either your son acts in a manner that suggests he is better than others, as did the boy in the preceding example, or he expresses weakness and vulnerability. In either case, parents, teachers and school counselors can help the victim learn ways to avoid the abuse.

5. Chores: How do you motivate kids to do their chores?

When I try to get my children to help around the house, they complain so much it almost seems easier to do things myself. I don't expect kids to like to work, but is there any way to improve their attitudes—at least a little? They are eleven and nine.

Your children are perfectly normal. Children in the middle years, from eight to twelve, look at requests with a what's-in-it-for-me attitude. What may appear selfish in an adult may be normal development in a child. This is not to say children should only do things they like to do, but it does tell us something about how best to deal with this age.

Studies in child development have shown that, before adolescence, children are not capable of putting themselves in the place of another. They cannot really understand what the other is feeling. The adolescent who constantly worries about what her friends think is actually demonstrating signs of a more advanced development. Your children have not yet reached this stage.

People are complex creatures, however, and children in the eight to twelve age range may often perform quite unselfish and generous acts. From early years children observe the people around them and imitate what they observe. Thus, a child who is exposed to the generosity of others may well display generous behavior himself. Imitation is a wonderful way to learn virtue.

As parents we can influence the behavior of the child from eight to twelve by taking her where she is. If what's-in-it-for-me is her normal orientation, you can offer concrete incentives within this frame for doing chores, studying or whatever behavior you are trying to encourage. Fairness, trade-offs and treats are all language the child understands.

Children place a high priority on fairness. Divide up jobs so that each does a fair share according to ability. Doing chores also offers a fine opportunity to rid yourself and your children of sexist stereotypes. Boys can do kitchen work and girls can do yard work. Work is work.

Build on your children's understanding of tit for tat. "If you do this for me, I'll do that for you" is the way they think. Mom might say, "If you cut the grass, Julie, I'll have time to make us a dessert for dinner." Or, "If you'll clean the family room, Tom, I'll go out and buy that volleyball set we've been meaning to get for some time." Show them how their help benefits everyone, themselves included.

Finally, almost everyone works better when there is a reward at the end of labor. Treats and rewards do not have to be considered bribes but rather *incentives*. We all need incentives. How many people would choose to work daily without the incentive of a paycheck?

An afternoon of yard work can be followed by a special cookout, a party to celebrate work well done. During summer vacation most children have free time. They can reasonably be expected to do more daily household chores than they do during the school year.

The treat for such extra work might be regular trips to the beach or going out to lunch once a week, perhaps with the whole family if such an excursion can be arranged.

A written chore list in the kitchen may serve your purpose. Usual chores include setting the table, washing the dishes, straightening or cleaning a room and washing the floors, woodwork or windows. Select one or two jobs and assign them at a family meeting. Alternate them monthly so no one gets bored. Follow my suggestions in Chapter Five for help with scheduling the chores and teaching your children how to do them.

Finally, keep track of the work done. All successful industries keep statistics. Somewhere, parents should have a record of all the work done, kept either in work units or time units. Follow my suggestions for charting in Chapter Four.

Charting, or keeping track, is important for two reasons: It programs the parent and the child. First, charts program the parent to notice and pay attention to the work done, changing the focus from the bad behavior to the good. Second, they program the child to learn a step-by-step completion of the job.

6. Clothing Expenses: How can we afford a teenage daughter?

Help! My teenage daughter is going to put us in the poorhouse. The problem is clothes. We have a moderate income, and I've always tried to keep food, clothing, vacations and all within our income. Now when we go shopping together the bills are out of proportion to the rest of our expenses. She is only fourteen, and at this rate I don't know how we'll survive through high school. How can we afford a teenage daughter?

Anyone who has ever been to a shopping mall knows that clothing is big business and expensive. It's even worse for teenagers. From early on, teens are aware that the exclusive models from fashionable boutiques are more desirable than mass-produced, mail-ordered clothing. Teens are often still growing and growth means more frequent new wardrobes. Any style, as dictated by the peer groups, changes frequently.

The easiest way for a family to survive teenage clothing, I've discovered, is to put the child in total charge of his or her expenses from the start of high school. The teenager's allowance should be substantial, but it covers (at least in our family) everything but room, board and medical expenses. (See "Allowances," p. 119.)

You determine how much the teen gets by estimating how much she needs and what she can afford. If you often shop with your daughter, you know how much clothes cost. In addition she will need personal and school expenses, entertainment, gifts and perhaps other items you can determine together. You and your teen should understand the amount starts on a trial basis and may need adjustment as you try out the system.

You can pay allowance weekly, monthly or several months at a time. A weekly allowance is easier to manage. An allowance at three-month intervals makes large purchases possible. (It's difficult to finance a new winter coat by the week.) My wife and I individualize the payment of allowances because we find that one child can handle three months' allowance and another would (and did!) use it up within a few days. In some cases we even keep the balance sheet ourselves and dole out the monthly allowance as needed. Don't be critical if your child cannot manage money over a long period; neither can many adults. Rather, help guide your child to learn how to handle money.

When you turn money management over to your children you must make some changes in your attitude. You might want them to buy at least one dressy outfit whereas they are happy with blue jeans exclusively. Independence means you respect their decisions about clothes. You can no longer pick up that cute little sales item and charge your daughter for it. If she is typical, she won't agree with your taste, and she won't want it. You can mention that a certain store is having a sale, but let her make the purchase.

If you get hand-me-downs from relatives or friends, the saving accrues to your child, not to you. Often this produces a changed attitude toward hand-me-downs. A slightly-used winter jacket looks more attractive to a teenager when it saves his allowance rather than your cash.

The advantages of this system are many. First, your teenager handles responsibility and learns from it. She learns clothing is important but is not a life-and-death matter. A poor purchase is a disappointment, but it is a fairly harmless way to learn from one's mistakes.

Most important, letting your child manage money takes much of the hassle out of the parent-teen relationship. Teens know exactly how much to expect from parents. If this is not sufficient to meet their needs or desires, they know that a part-time job, and not pestering parents, is the next alternative. Your child might tell you wistfully that his buddy just asks and his mom gives him a dollar; deep down, however, he knows that asking for money is juvenile and managing money is adult.

Last but not least, your own budget benefits because you know, for better or worse, the exact cost of living with a teen.

7. Companions: Can I pick my children's friends?

I am the mother of eight children ranging in age from eight to sixteen. Our children go to school with all types of children. I have tried to teach them that each person is a child of God and should be respected. But how am I supposed to draw the line about associating with certain children whose background is immoral? One neighbor lives unwed with a man and her six children; two of these children (ages fifteen and sixteen) are pregnant and unmarried. And what about the child who proudly tells of smoking pot or taking drugs, or the one who proudly brags of premarital sexual relations?

Do I teach the way to live, try to give good examples and then leave it up to God to guide my teens in their companions?

"Avoid bad companions" is not nearly so clear and simple a directive as the old examination of conscience would indicate.

First, how do you judge a "bad companion"? Certainly we don't agree with the native bigotry which proclaims Catholic kids are good; all others are bad. We also should recognize that people who look, dress or talk differently from us are not bad. Adults often decide that people who lie, cheat, steal and abuse sex are "bad." Yet we know that terrible injustices can be committed by well-dressed business executives enjoying their twenty-dollar business lunches.

In general, when I have little concrete information, I give each person the benefit of the doubt. If my child likes this person, I think he must have recognized something good and admirable which I perhaps have not noticed.

On the other hand, I draw the line at companions who brag about drugs and premarital sex. Pre-adolescents and young adolescents are highly susceptible to peer influences. If the companions are a couple of years older, as often happens, their actions can take on a glamorous or heroic cast. As far as I am concerned, that is an influence I do not wish to tolerate.

I do not attempt to play God and judge whether these

people are bad. I simply decide that I do not want their influences on my children.

How do you deal with unwanted companions? The direct approach says, "You may never play with the Jones children." The Jones children, being off limits, become even more glamorous and interesting than before. Furthermore, if a daughter ever wishes to irritate her mother a bit, she can raise the issue, "Why can't I play with Susie Jones?" Long fruitless discussions ensue.

An indirect approach usually works better. Encourage those friendships of which you approve. If one child persists in an attraction to the undesirable companion, try to make the association impossible: "It's too late to visit Susie" or "We're doing something else at that time."

Probably the most effective way to deal with your children's companions is to encourage all your children to bring their friends to your house. If possible set up a pool table or ping-pong table. Have board games available. Make your home an attractive place to bring friends.

Hospitality naturally involves extra noise, extra food and extra confusion. Of course, as parents of eight children you are probably somewhat immune to noise. And peanut butter sandwiches and popcorn make acceptable, and cheap, snacks.

For a conscientious parent, the advantages of having teenagers at home far outweigh the inconveniences. You know where your children are and with whom. If certain companions are questionable, you can get to know them better. Even children you don't approve of can be made welcome within your home. When you control the atmosphere, it is doubtful they will exert so "bad" an influence.

Home is a safe place for your children to learn that there are all kinds of people in the world. Also, other people can share the wholesome, loving atmosphere of your home. Perhaps most important of all, you teach by your own example that warm, loving hospitality is truly a Christian virtue.

8. Dating: What are some good guidelines for teen dating?

I would like some practical advice about setting hours and regulating dating behavior for teenagers. I believe in giving increasing freedom as they get older, but what are some good guidelines at thirteen, sixteen and eighteen?

In the 1950's Robert Paul Smith wrote a book entitled *"Where Did You Go?" "Out." "What Did You Do?" "Nothing."* (New York: W. W. Norton, 1957). Although written about younger children, that title sums up the conversation that frequently occurs between parents and teen.

Formal dating for many teens is practically nonexistent today. A group of boys or girls drives around in a car, looking for members of the opposite sex. They stop at a drive-in or a pizza place for food and conversation. They go out, but they do not date formally. The old rule, "You may date at sixteen but not before," is not relevant for today's teens.

Furthermore, the mobility provided by a car means it is virtually impossible for you the parent to know where your teen is at night. Even a well-meaning teen cannot tell his parent where he will be. He is simply "out."

Despite this casual style of recreation, it is possible for you to set and apply guidelines. Here are three ways:

1) *Learn about community practices.* I am not advocating that you go by the old teen argument, "Everybody's doing it." On the other hand, to ignore what other children in the community do is to overlook valuable guidelines. Other parents also wish to bring up their children well and safely. If other children are allowed to follow certain practices, you can probably let your child do so. If the seventh- and eighth-graders frequent a certain local movie house on Friday nights, if the junior high holds dances once a month, if high school dances last until midnight, it is probably all right for your child to participate in these activities.

2) *See for yourself what is going on.* If you are undecided about letting your sixth- or seventh-grader attend school dances, offer to chaperone. You will probably be warmly welcomed (the job is not much in demand), and you can unobtrusively learn what junior high social life is about.

3) *Use common sense to make rules that are clear and fair.* Since teens frequently do ride around or go from one place to another in the course of an evening, regulating hours is much more effective than trying to regulate where your child goes. Ten o'clock is an appropriate deadline through eighth grade, eleven o'clock for high school freshmen and sophomores and midnight for juniors and seniors. These hours can be modified for special occasions, but they are appropriate curfews for my community. The practices of your community may vary.

Once a child graduates from high school, my wife and I no longer set hours. The child is an adult and expected to be responsible for his or her own hours.

9. Defiance: What can you do with a teen who won't listen?

How do you handle a sixteen-year-old girl who knows it all and is self-bent on destruction? She refuses to listen. Her choice of companions is deplorable and her school marks are failing.

She has no respect for anyone, herself included. She seems to be anti-Church, anti-teachers, anti-police, anti-all authority. Her talk is vulgar. Hostility reigns.

The Bible says: Love, love, love. It is not working. I think she has even tried marijuana. We continue to give her a good example and are storming heaven with our prayers, but to no avail yet. I'm about nuts.

Some children test, challenge, resist and blatantly defy authority. Dr. James Dobson, in his book *Parenting Isn't for Cowards* (Waco, Texas: Word Books, 1987), reports that such strong-willed children may outnumber compliant ones by as many as three to one.

What is happening today? Anthropologists tell us that society raises the type of children it needs. They speculate that we need more brash, brave young adults who can adapt readily to rapid changes. The fact that young girls appear to be leading the way may reflect society's need for more assertive women.

This fact, however, is hard on parents. You have described a teen with passionate eloquence, including your own intense frustration.

There are two basic parental strategies for rebellious teens. The first is to try to keep increasing the punishment until you achieve compliance. The second is to make an effort to redirect the strong energies of the teen into more acceptable channels.

I would avoid punitive strategy for the main reason that it probably won't work. Even if it does, it may be at the expense of your teen's drive and self-confidence.

Here are a few hints on the second strategy, how to direct and control without destroying the drive and energy.

1) Don't take her words too seriously. Teens often use strong words in an absolute sense to shock. Pay more attention to what she does than what she says.

2) Don't confront. Avoid getting into situations where it's your mouth against hers. This tends to reinforce her mouthiness and to escalate the verbal battles.

3) As much as possible, ignore her mouth. Ignoring is not doing nothing. Ignoring is a powerful way to get rid of undesirable behavior.

4) Focus on compliance in realistic and important areas such as curfew, school grades, chores and freedom from drug use. Use charts to reward her progress. Mark down when she comes home on time, completes a chore or gets a good grade. Keep track of her good behavior rather than her misbehavior. See Chapter Four for help on charting.

5) Allow her peer friendships, unless they are clearly destructive. Teens gain more strength from peers than any other source. Use teen groupings and friendships rather than fight them. Encourage parties in your home, overnights and other group experiences with acceptable teens.

6) Talk with other parents of teens. Realize that you are not alone. You may even provide an occasional time-out for one another by trading or taking in a temporarily defiant teen.

7) Hang in there. Take comfort from the fact that most youngsters will return to their family values once adolescence is over. As Dobson says, parenting is not for cowards. The defiant teen is a child of our times. Be patient with your teen and yourself, value her energy and learn ways to redirect it.

10. Failing Math: How can I help Johnny with his math?

My son is in fifth grade this year. He has just barely passed the last two years. He does well enough in his other subjects but seems to have a mental block about numbers. I am worried that he will get so far behind that he'll fail math. Would you recommend I help him at home? How?

Good for you. Better to be concerned ahead of time and prevent trouble than to have to remedy a failure. Yes, there are things you can do at home to help with math.

Basic math facts, like spelling and vocabulary, can be tedious. If your child is tired of school and turned off by failure, it may tax your ingenuity to keep him interested. The challenge is to make math homework interesting and fun. Try to keep it brief and different in style from classroom work.

Repetition and speed drills are unavoidable in learning

basic math facts. Here are some ways to make drilling less tedious.

1) Flash cards are a proven way of learning basic math facts. Let your son make them, using three-by-five index cards. He should write the multiplication, division or fraction problem with marker on the front and the answer on the back. Letting your son help prepare the materials is in itself a learning experience.

   Shuffle the cards and present them one at a time to him. Place those he gets right in a pile to his right. Count correct answers by giving him a raisin or peanut for each one. Place the cards he gets wrong at the bottom of the deck. Repeat them until he gets them correct. As he improves, use a stopwatch for speed drills.

   For a change, let him give the cards to you. To make it more difficult, limit your time to answer to one or two seconds.

2) Calculators, computers and video games help a person learn math. If your son enjoys video games, he may warm to having his math facts presented in this fashion. Review the games available in your local store; choose those emphasizing math skills.

3) Playing family store is still another way to learn basic math. Let your son collect canned goods from your cabinets along with various other household items. He should make up a price for each and put them on a shelf behind him.

   You can then shop at his store. Addition, subtraction and multiplication are needed as you purchase one or more items. You can ask him to compute sales tax, calculate the refund for an item returned, determine the price of a single item which was priced three for $1.19, compute the price per ounce of different items and determine the best buy.

   In short, you can be a very difficult customer. He can total his sales and balance his cash at the end of the business day.

11. Family Meal: How can we get our family to eat together?

We read about how important it is for a family to eat together. If that is the case, then our family is surely in trouble. I don't think we have a single meal together during the week.

My husband is off to work before our two children get down for breakfast. I work a thirty-hour week and have lunch at the office. Our two middle-school-aged children are rarely home from paper route, band practice or sports practice in time for us to eat dinner together as a family. What can we do?

Your situation is all too typical: a family of four pulled every which way by society. No wonder families are having trouble when the members no longer find it possible to share even a meal.

You are right to be concerned about eating together. The importance of sharing a meal as community is emphasized throughout the Bible (see Exodus 12; Luke 22:14-20; and Luke 24:28-31 for a few examples). Eating is one of these few and vital functions that serves to bind the participants together. People who eat together are more apt to maintain close relationships with one another.

What can you do? Let's analyze your situation. If you are not eating together as a family, then one or more of the family members is busy doing something else. School activities or job are taking priority over family. You may say that family comes first, but if you are never together for meals, then I think you should question your own statement.

Be practical. Sometimes you should try to put family first. There are twenty-one meals in most weeks. You ought to be able to find a way to share some of them together as a family. Some meals together are better than none.

What about breakfast? Can Dad get to work a bit later on one day? Can your children get up earlier one day per week? Have a special breakfast treat. Set the table and do some of the meal preparation the night before. What about a Saturday brunch or a meal on Sunday after church? A little ingenuity plus a sense that family has priority can turn breakfast into a special meal.

If lunch is out during the week, what about weekends? Can you have a special lunch on Saturday or Sunday? Keep it simple and short enough so that it is enjoyed by all. It is more important that it happens regularly every week.

Since dinner time is the usual family meal, you may want to set aside one evening per week when the family meal comes ahead of sports practices, jobs or any social engagement. Plan a special menu. If members cannot make the regular dinner hour, you might arrange for a late evening meal once a week. Have a festive atmosphere as you sit down together, European-style, at eight or nine in the evening.

Snacks also offer an opportunity to eat together. Make an effort to plan a mini-meal during a favorite television program you watch together or allow some time before bed for a family get-together for snacks and conversations.

Eating together nowadays often requires special planning. For a family trying to stay close, however, it is important enough to warrant the extra trouble and planning.

12. Fears: How does a child master fear?

My daughter, five years old, is very fearful. She's afraid to go upstairs by herself, downstairs by herself, and so on. She started holding on to my clothing in the house, holding my hands and wanting me to hold her. I took her to see Rocky III, *which was rated PG, and she said that scared her, but the fear was there before the movie.*

There was a time when I was afraid of everything, and I know I passed it on to her. With the help of God and other caring people I am dealing with fear. But how do I help her?

Five-year-olds commonly develop fears. Reflect on what they are going through. Sometimes for the first time they are leaving their homes, making new friends, meeting other adults and starting school. The unknown frequently arouses apprehension.

You may not have passed on your own fearfulness to your daughter. Just as likely, the fears you describe are part of her own development.

What to do? Reassurance from you will help, but apparently it is not enough. Nevertheless, you can remind her occasionally that she has nothing to fear. Perhaps you can share that you too were afraid when you were five.

The best reassurance is not verbal but physical. Your daughter knows that. She wants to hold your hand and cling to your clothing.

Don't hesitate to take the initiative and accompany her to strange and scary places. You may want to lie down with her in her bed for a while until she relaxes and falls asleep.

You can help her detach a little from you by giving her something of yours to carry with her. A small photo of you or an item of your clothing would be good.

The best strategy, however, is gradually to give her control over her fears. Stop giving her lectures on the futility of fears. Try a few games.

"Name the monster" often helps. You and your daughter might brainstorm a few funny names for the worst of them. "Uncle Charley," "Ugly Ogre" and "Bad Old Barney" are a lot easier to deal with than a vague unknown. The funnier, the better. If your daughter starts to laugh, she will be halfway over her fear.

"Silly poems" can also help. Make them up with your daughter. "Bogey monster, dark and scary, I think I'll hit you with a cherry." The child can repeat the poem in fearsome moments. She has something to do rather than simply be afraid.

"Draw the fear" is another useful game. One preschool girl sat down beside her mother and drew all the frightening things they could imagine. They taped the pictures to her walls and closet door "so you know what to worry about." Somehow the fears no longer seemed so terrifying.

Finally, you might want to give your daughter a

night-light. Let her control its use. She can turn it on whenever she needs it. She may use it for a long time. Eventually she will be content to know that by turning on the light she can make the fears go away by herself. A transistor radio can serve the same purpose.

By accepting the fear you demonstrate to your daughter that you hear and understand her. By giving her control through naming, humor and night-lights, you help her master her fears herself and that mastery boosts her self-esteem. After all, mastery is a grown-up skill.

13. Hyperactivity: How do you handle a hyperactive child?

We have a four-year-old son who is into everything. He can't sit still and he is a terror around the house. He talks constantly, teases his two sisters, accidentally breaks almost all his toys and is slowly driving me crazy. My neighbor says he is hyperactive and that I should see my physician. What do you think?

The word *hyperactive* has two meanings, one very general and one a specific medical diagnosis. In general, hyperactive means overly active. Your son is certainly that. It sounds as though you have your hands full. The treatment possibilities can be summarized by the three Ds: drugs, diet and discipline.

Medically, *hyperactive* refers to uncontrolled behavior caused by a neurological problem. Nerve impulses are not adequately controlled. The child is unable to learn in school or to perform athletically because he cannot control his energy.

If the problem is physical, the child may respond well to drugs such as Ritalin or Cylert. Although these drugs would "speed up" an adult, they serve to control the unchecked nerve impulses of a hyperactive child. These drugs take effect within a few hours. If the hyperactivity is physically caused, you will know within twenty-four to forty-eight hours because your child will be noticeably calmer with the drugs.

Tranquilizers have also been used with some success to treat hyperactivity in children. Valium is perhaps the most common one. Drugs, however, should be used as a last resort and only where the problem has been shown to be physically based. Drugs have too many side effects. They can also mask other problems.

Diet is another, safer way of treating hyperactivity. Diet seems to work in some cases and not in others. Dr. Benjamin Feingold in his book, *Why Your Child Is Hyperactive* (New York, New York: Random House, 1985), recommends eliminating all foods with synthetic food coloring, flavoring and additives. Other allergists systematically eliminate certain foods such as dairy products, chocolate and refined sugar. They find that when these foods are eliminated, the hyperactive child improves. In any case, finding the culprits in diet requires detective-like observation on your part. If you are fortunate enough to find a physician who works with diet and hyperactivity, you will have a helpful adviser in a complicated situation.

Discipline is the third D. It is the least radical and most difficult approach of the three. It takes parental time and attention to discipline well. Good discipline requires consistency and follow-through. The parent cannot say something and then fail to enforce it. For this reason, good discipline usually does not try to cover everything. Rather, parents select those few areas which are most important to them and where they feel they can be most effective. A lot of growing-up behavior (running, spilling, noise and so on) can be ignored.

Good discipline requires that at least as much time be spent in rewarding good behavior as in punishing bad. Let me give a few simple suggestions on how you might apply these principles to your son.

You might begin by selecting one behavior he does well and one he does that you feel he must stop. Discuss these with his father. Be very clear in your minds what behavior you wish to encourage and what behavior you wish to stop. Also, be clear on what you will use as a reward and what will be the penalty. Don't try to do too much.

Let us suppose you feel you must begin by stopping his teasing and bullying of his sisters. When he teases, tell him firmly to stop. If the teasing continues another sixty seconds, physically remove him from the scene. Set him in a chair. If he won't stay, *gently* sit on him to make him stay just long enough for the bad behavior to stop. Then let him go again. Even a minute or two can seem like an eternity to an overactive child.

What do you reward? With all that energy, he must be doing something good. Suggest that he straighten the living room daily and reward him with your attention. Let him talk into a tape recorder for five minutes and then hear himself. Even more simply, if he likes to talk, take time to talk to him. Talking is certainly a valued skill, as any parent whose child is late to talk will be quick to tell you.

You have a real task with your four-year-old. Get out of the house to refresh yourself when you feel you need it. In dealing with him, try discipline and diet. If that does not work, see your physician about the possibility of using drug therapy. Good luck!

14. Junk Food: How can I control the consumption of junk food?

I am concerned about the amount of junk food my children eat, particularly sweets. Although I try to serve only a reasonable amount of sweet things at home, they get sweets from friends and neighbors and buy sweets with their allowances. How can I control junk food?

You are right. Sweets are everywhere. Children get many sweets outside the home. Even schools and doctors' offices sometimes give out sweets as rewards. What's a parent to do?

You can try to enlist the cooperation of your friends and neighbors. Suggest treats you welcome for your children rather than criticizing the foods they have been offering. Since you cannot control the behavior of your neighbors and since you probably do not wish to break up a friendship over this matter, this approach is limited to suggestion.

Basically your control over sweets lies mainly within your home. Most eating is done at home so your efforts can make a real difference in your family's nutrition. As in other areas of behavior, you can try a negative approach, a positive approach or a combination of the two.

The negative approach is to ban sweets, trying at the same time to educate your children as to why sweets are undesirable. In my experience, this approach is valid but only moderately successful. Occasionally I have met a child so well schooled in nutrition that he will refuse sweets remarking, "My mother won't let me have that. That's not good for me." I have met very few children like this, however, and certainly my own children would never make such a remark!

Limiting sweets can be done by a time or money limit. For example, limit your child to spending only twenty-five cents a week on sweets or to buying sweets only on Saturday morning, the usual allowance day. Such practices can lead to numerous questions ("Is a week up yet?" "Does sugar cereal count as a sweet?" "Can two of us go together and buy a can of pop?"). You want to avoid the discussions resulting from such questions because they focus so much attention on buying-sweets behavior and they wear you down.

Another way of limiting sweets at home is to set a limit for yourself. Resolve to serve a sweet dessert only once per week. Such a limit helps *you* to kick the sweets habit and makes you feel virtuous rather than guilty when the cookie jar is empty. Another effective way to limit junk foods is simply to get them out of the house. Your children cannot eat what is not available.

The positive side of handling junk food is more challenging, more creative and more fun. The important rule to follow is: *Eliminate the sweets but not the treats.* The good foods you can turn into treats include fruits, nuts, seeds, grains and dairy products. When shopping, consider buying a treat food from these categories. Nuts in the shell are a fun project for children. Peanuts are good but rather commonplace. Cashews, pistachio nuts and sunflower seeds are a bit more exotic. Popcorn is a nutritious grain which is also fun for children to make as well as eat.

Dairy products can be used in many ways. Make exotic drinks using the blender. Try yogurt or cottage cheese dips for fresh vegetables. Buy new kinds of cheeses for the family to try. For a super treat, buy a fruit out of season—strawberries in January, watermelon in February—and serve it with the enthusiasm it deserves.

When fruits are in season, freeze your own fruits without sugar. Peaches, berries and applesauce freeze well with no sugar at all.

The advertising for junk food often emphasizes that these foods are treats. They belong with good times and celebrations, the ads imply. Try this same technique when you provide nutritious treats for your family. Serve desserts with a flair. Develop your own original combinations of fruits for dessert. Top each serving with a little coconut or a maraschino cherry. Invent suitable names for your desserts. Why serve fruit when you can offer "Mama's melon melange" or "Red, white and blueberries"?

15. Lateness: How can I get my son to show up on time?

My nine-year-old son has his head in the clouds. I send him off to school in our small town, concerned about whether he will get there on time, if at all. On the way he has to step in every puddle, pet every dog, gawk at every cloud in the sky and crisscross every backyard.

After school it's worse. He gets home eventually, but sometimes he manages to appear in the strangest and most faraway places. Often enough, he is late for supper and I have a hard time tracking him down.

I worry that he may wander into trouble. I would also like to have him home for supper on time without having to comb the neighborhood.

Thank you for so vividly describing a common occurrence: the odyssey of Mr. Slowpoke. Your son, like so many of his act-alikes, lives in another world, untroubled by the deadlines and details that bother you and me.

Yes, you need to get him to school on time. And he needs to be home for family supper. He will have to move along a bit to get where he is supposed to be, when he is supposed to be there.

Before I suggest a plan, however, recognize that wandering has its bright side. Curiosity, wonder and awe are all gifts to be cultivated. Too often we adults are in such a hurry to get someplace we think is so important that we forget to stop and smell the flowers.

So let's try to cure him of his lateness, but not his curious mind and meandering feet. How can you get him to school and home again on time?

If it is an option for you, I would walk with him to school in the morning. Walking with him has many advantages. He gets there on time, so it is good discipline because it is effective. Further, you have the opportunity to model on-time behavior. He learns by accompanying you.

There are advantages for you as well. You can relearn how to watch for puddles and wonder about the clouds. Also, you will be starting the day with the healthiest exercise of all, a brisk walk.

If you cannot or choose not to walk to school with your son, ask a neighbor or adult friend you and your son trust to walk with him. Or let the school handle his lateness. They have a regular policy for tardy youngsters. Don't intervene to protect or excuse him.

Consequences are also one way to handle lateness for supper. Set a time to be home, perhaps 5:30. You might even give him an inexpensive wristwatch. If he is not home by 5:30, then he has a consequence. Washing dishes, no television and early bedtime are popular penalties.

A better way might be to motivate him to be home on time. Keep a chart of his check-in times. Just like workers, he can clock in each day after school. Perhaps a special food treat would be available until 5:30, but not afterward.

Or keep a chart with daily smile faces for every evening he is home on time. Five smile faces might earn a certain desired reward.

The clocking in, the food treat and the charting are positive ways to increase his motivation to be home on time. They usually work better than penalties because they focus on the good behavior rather than the bad.

Good luck in getting your wanderer home. I hope he gets there on time but never forgets there are clouds to watch and dogs to pet.

16. Losing: How do I help my child recover from losses?

Every competitor—and every parent of a competitor— dreams of a moment of glory: the come-from-behind finish as the underdog beats the favored runner; the brilliant piano solo which wins first-place honors.

But in any given competition, most of the participants will be losers. One individual or one team wins. All the rest lose.

When a competitor loses to a better performer in a good contest, he or she at least may have the satisfaction of a good try. More disappointing is the frustration that results when fate dashes long-cherished hopes: The swimmer who has been practicing all through high school develops an ear infection just before the biggest meet of senior year; the voice student gets a throat infection on the eve of a major competition.

Such reversals are bitter blows. Life seems unfair. At these moments children need their parents.

In helping a child cope with disappointment, it is easier to give advice about what parents should not do. Do not deny the disappointment with remarks such as "It's all right," or "It wasn't important anyway" or "Don't feel bad." The parents wish to spare the child disappointment. Denying the failure and the feelings of failure, however, is a lie. The event was important. The defeat is not all right.

Parents cannot control that part of the child's world or the accompanying feelings.

Furthermore, do not criticize the opposition in an attempt to uplift your child's spirits.

"Their team practices three times a day. No wonder they won."

"That school recruits athletes. They don't even live within the school district."

Avoid sour grapes. Do not teach your child that he or she is so superior and perfect that a loss must be due to the dishonesty of the opposition.

Do not make excuses.

"You would have won easily if you weren't just coming off a bout with the flu."

"The referees were terrible."

Such remarks imply that losing is so unthinkable, it must be justified in some way.

What *can* you do? First, be sympathetic and supportive. Does your daughter feel so bad that she cries over the loss of a race? There is no shame in tears. You don't know what to say? Then don't say anything. Just hug her.

Second, let your child express frustration and grief, but don't emphasize it. Sometimes the youngster is a poor sport. He blames the referees or makes other excuses for himself. At this time it is best to ignore the negative remarks. Good sportsmanship can be learned, but the moment of defeat is no time for a lecture or a formal lesson. Talking about the poor sportsmanship only draws attention to it.

Third, compliment signs of good losing. Say something like, "I was proud of the way you played after missing that free throw." It is one thing to make an error. It is another to bounce right back. "I notice you congratulated the winner. That's class."

Fourth, once a child has expressed disappointment, applaud all positive attitudes and new goals.

Son: "We'll get 'em next year."

Dad: "You bet you will."

Winning is glorious. Losing can be bitter. But losing is

also an opportunity to learn to cope with life. Children who learn to take a defeat with grace are growing toward maturity.

17. Lying: Why do children lie and what can parents do?

My husband and I are feeling betrayed and hopeless because our sixteen-year-old daughter lies to us. She seems sincere, but on several occasions we found out later that everything she said was untrue. I fear we cannot be close as a family if we cannot trust each other. Is this behavior likely to pass? Is there anything we can do?

You describe well a parent's feelings of dismay. "How can a child return love and caring by lying? Can we ever restore a good family relationship?"

Most often a child lies to keep from getting in trouble. Another reason may be to get her way. As a teenager might put it: "If I told you the truth, you wouldn't let me do what I wanted." These reasons do not excuse lying but help to recognize why it might occur.

Lying frustrates parents like no other misbehavior because lying is totally within the child's control. The usual suggestions about rewarding good behavior and disciplining misbehavior do not work with lying because parents do not even know when the misbehavior is occurring.

The parent's only recourse is to take away the payoff for lying. If lying works for the child, it is likely to continue. Verify everything from other sources. Is Lisa staying overnight with her girlfriend? Call the girlfriend's parent.

Has Larry skipped school and lied when you questioned him? Contact the school counselor and set up a program to check on and discipline attendance. Call the counselor personally whenever your child is going to be absent.

Does Tim come home after curfew with the excuse: "We had a flat tire"? Establish that curfew is curfew. If he is late because of a misfortune, sympathize but impose the penalty anyway. You will have taken away the reason to make up an excuse.

When some activity cannot be verified from another source ignore it.

"Where were you?"

"We went to a movie."

In most cases the parent cannot verify this. Of course, you could grill the child: "What time did the movie start? Tell me the plot."

Such questioning focuses time and attention on lying. Ideally, you want to ignore lying. Ignoring is an effective way to stop behavior. There is no point in continuing to do something when you get no response. Will lying stop eventually? Some adolescents who lie grow into adults who are very open and honest with their parents. While no one can predict the future, human behavior suggests that lying will stop most quickly when it proves useless and is ignored.

Some parents try to "nail" a lying child by setting him up. They get evidence from outside sources, let the child lie, then confront him with the facts. While such a practice may give the parent a grim satisfaction, it destroys every shred of the child's self-respect. It is the cruelest of put-downs and leaves the child no way out. For these reasons it is not a good way to handle lying.

18. Messy Rooms: What can I do when no one picks up anything?

You'll probably think this is trivial, but it is a real problem for me. I have three children, ages eight, eleven and thirteen, who must be the worst litterers in the state. I get after them to pick up their things, sometimes I even take away a privilege until they pick up. My husband is more tolerant. He says I should just relax about it. Is the problem inevitable?

Don't apologize for your question. You find disorder hard to live with. That's legitimate. You are entitled to speak up. There are several approaches you can try.

1) Explain the problem and try to enlist your child's cooperation. Do I hear you laughing? You should be. This is probably the least effective choice you can make for the age you are dealing with.

   First, your children don't see a littered house as a problem. Second, assisting another person because you understand her problem and difficulty is a fairly sophisticated, adult response. Children the ages of yours do not feel empathy for you because they are too young to have reached this stage of growth in human relationships.

2) You can remind them every time they litter. In practice this habit would become nagging. You will get frustrated from repeating yourself constantly, your children will tune you out and the problem will remain.

3) You can give your children incentives to pick up by offering rewards for performance or punishments for failure. You already allude to having used part of this technique when you say you have sometimes taken away privileges until they pick up. Incentives are a very effective way to change behavior.

   Success with this method depends on the time and attention you are willing to devote to it. You must follow through on your plan. For example, you might decide that each child should pick up one room daily before dinner. However, when one child is late getting home because of a piano lesson and the rest of the family must rush dinner to attend an early evening meeting, the plan needs to be flexible enough to handle these contingencies.

Despite the difficulties, don't overlook the possibilities in this method. If you choose it, set very specific conditions and keep the plan simple enough to oversee it consistently. If you must become a full-time bookkeeper to record successes and failures, the plan will be more trouble than it is worth. Follow my suggestions in Chapter Four for charting to change behavior.

4) Structure the environment. Simple as it sounds, it is easier to put things away when there is a place for everything. Organize your house so that family members know where things go. A box for each child's papers and books, and a labeled hook for coats and hats may help a lot. The proper location for books, sports equipment and clothing should be close to the normal traffic flow. Few children will cross the entire house to put an item in its proper place. As much as possible, bring the place to the child, not the child to the place.

5) Finally, if getting your children to pick up is more trouble than it is worth and litter is getting you down, do it yourself. You need not carefully restore everyone's possessions to perfect order. Designate one large junk drawer for odds and ends left around. Put a big box in an inconspicuous location. At pickup time, put all big things in the box and little things in the junk drawer. Period. The house is picked up, and the owners know where to find their belongings.

The sheer inconvenience of hunting for their things might improve the children's behavior. Your desire for order will be satisfied. And the whole problem will get neither more nor less attention than it deserves.

19. Mischievous Toddlers: How can I make my toddler behave?

I have a problem with my daughter who is eighteen months old. I find myself constantly spanking her because she will not obey simple commands like: "Come here," "Stay out" (of drawers, cupboards, etc.) and "Don't scream" (she loves to hear herself scream, I think). She just stands there saying "no" or completely ignores me. First, I ask her nicely, but by the fourth or fifth time, my patience has left and I am harsh with her.

I realize I am not a patient person. So far I've only spanked her, but I hate myself terribly afterward. Why can't I go just one day without spanking or hollering at her? Am I sick? After all she is only a baby and she should be happy, and full of smiles and laughter. She is when she's around her father.

I love her so much and I want her to grow up happy and wanting to be with her parents, come home for visits and have fond childhood memories. These are things I don't have. I couldn't bear it if I lost both my parents and my child. My husband and I get along very well and he is great with her. I hope you can help me before it is too late.

Thank you for your vivid account. You clearly point out that life with young children is not all sweetness and roses. I certainly do not think it is too late. I see some real strengths in you and you can build on these to become a good parent.

Despite an unhappy childhood, you are coping as an adult. You recognize you are not patient. Each of us has developed different personality traits. It is not the tendency to impatience which is wrong but acting on that impatience in ways that hurt others. You are distressed because you spank your baby all the time. Let's take the situations you describe and choose other means of discipline.

First, she won't "come here." An eighteen-month-old child is at the very earliest stage of discipline. Although toddlers know a few words, they are basically physical creatures. Thus, to be effective you make all your discipline physical but without spanking. In this case, when you say "come here," simply go get her. At age three or four she will come in response to your verbal commands, but not yet.

Second, she won't stay out of drawers, cupboards and so on. An eighteen-month-old sees no reason to stay out of the most fascinating places in the home. There is no way you can convince her that staying out is desirable. One way might be to involve fear of dire punishment, a course you do not wish to take. A better way is to childproof. Tie cabinets together. Lock them. Put valuable things up high. If she loves pots and pans, let her play with them. They are the cheapest, most sturdy toys around. Getting into everything is perfectly normal for a toddler, and it passes as she grows older.

Third, she won't stop screaming. Everyone from the littlest baby to the oldest senior citizen loves attention. Your daughter has discovered how to get it. If you really want her to stop, the most effective course is to ignore it. The screaming will not disappear immediately, but if it draws no attention, it is much less fun. No attention, no screaming.

Finally, schedule time for yourself, even if brief intervals are all you manage. Hire a high school girl to come in for an hour after school, and take a walk or bicycle ride alone. Let your husband take your daughter on a shopping trip or a picnic occasionally and you stay home in your silent house.

20. Night-waking: How do you get a child to sleep through the night?

Our sixteen-month-old little boy has rarely slept all night since he was six months old. We put him on a full-size mattress on the floor beside our bed and for two nights he slept all night. When we put the mattress into a frame, he woke up several times and would only sleep with us. He has two sisters, ages eight and four. I've tried letting the oldest one sleep with him, putting the mattress on the floor and giving him medicine for worms. Nothing works. I am pregnant again and wonder how we can help him sleep alone. Our doctor says he is spoiled and should be allowed to cry. I just can't do that. He seems only semi-awake and cries like he is scared. We also have a lot of pressure put on us because he sleeps with us.

You are obviously parents who are centered on your baby's needs. Your letter does not ask "How can I get a good night's sleep?" (although I'm sure you would enjoy one), but rather, "How can I help my baby?" There is a world of difference between the two approaches. Your approach leads to meeting the child's needs.

Sleep problems are more common than most parents admit. The first question most new parents hear is "Is he/she a good baby?" The next question explains what is meant by *good*: "Does he/she sleep through the night?"

Most infants in human history have slept with their siblings. Night-waking by children and adults was considered normal and natural. No one was supposed to sleep through the night. Always another person was close by for comfort.

In our culture, however, people are expected to sleep alone and sleep well. Babies a few weeks old are bedded alone and expected to sleep through the night. If an older child such as your sixteen-month-old does not sleep through the night, he is "spoiled." Yet a wife may find that when her husband is away overnight, she does not sleep well. Interestingly, a wakeful child is spoiled. A wakeful adult has insomnia.

You need the support of other parents who believe that meeting a child's needs is not spoiling but parenting. You need the reassurance that other parents *do* get up night after night and that, eventually, the child will become a better sleeper—if he is not made anxious by being pushed. I suggest you contact the La Leche League (9616 Minneapolis Ave., Franklin Park, IL 60131) for a list of their literature and the location of a support group in your area.

21. Parental Anger: How can I control my own temper?

"I get so mad at my two-year-old, and she's only a baby!"

"Sometimes I think my son does that just to get me mad."

"You know that will make your father angry."

Face it—parents get mad at their children. Usually, anger amounts to a mild form of irritation and impatience. Sometimes anger can be much more serious, leading to deep frustration and even child abuse. Parents need ways to cope with anger. Here are some effective techniques for short-fused parents:

1) If you have a low frustration level and fear you might lose control and abuse your child, then never spank. For you, spanking, even "love pats," are out when you are angry. At the same time do not substitute mean words which can abuse a child's spirit as badly as striking abuses the body. And do not substitute long lectures to your child.

2) Learn to control outcomes. If your child won't come when called, go get him. If your children are fighting, separate them. If your child is too noisy, send him outside or buy earplugs. Use non-spanking disciplines: Ignore bad behavior; childproof where possible; limit the number of demands you make of your children.

3) Make a conscious effort to touch in affection. Put your arm around your child when you read to her or watch TV together. Rock him in a rocking chair. Invite him to snuggle in your bed for a few moments in the morning as a lovely warm way to start the day. Be generous with spontaneous hugs and kisses during the day.

4) Depend on others; you need them. Let your spouse spend as much time as possible with your child. Let your child spend brief periods with relatives or friends. Trade with neighbors. Four- and five-year-olds often play better

when a friend visits than they do alone. Indeed, two children are actually easier to tend than one.

5) Schedule time for yourself. Some parents are relaxed and easygoing. They enjoy having the children around all the time. Others get frustrated easily and need time for themselves. Recognize your own strengths and limitations. If you need time out, take it. Hire a school child to babysit after school. Take your children to story hour at your local library and enjoy the time for yourself. Plan short breaks for yourself before you get desperate.

6) Examine your own goals and life-style to find out the reason you get frustrated easily. Frequently, adults who are extremely productive and time-conscious are most easily frustrated. They are so aware of the "important adult things" they have to do that they cannot easily adjust to the slower, relaxed pace which suits children. Perhaps you want uninterrupted time to write, sew, build furniture or do ceramics. It helps to realize that these options will be more available as your children get older. Meanwhile, you might select less ambitious personal projects that can survive interruptions and even be set aside for periods of time. As long-time mothers will tell you, "Your children are little for such a short time. Don't miss their growing up."

7) Find some good models of parenting. Look for a neighbor or friend who seems to have happy children and enjoys being a parent. Share your feelings with her. Ask questions. Formerly we learned parenting by watching our own mothers, aunts, uncles and cousins raise their families. Nowadays that option is rarely available. Find your own confidantes. La Leche League promotes "good mothering through breast feeding." It is open to you even if you are not nursing and offers an excellent opportunity for mother-to-mother sharing. Parent effectiveness groups and community parents groups are also sources for sharing your feelings about parenting and learning what children are like at various ages and stages.

22. Piano Lessons: How do I get my child to practice the piano?

My eight-year-old son would like to take piano lessons. Is this a good age to start? How can I keep him interested enough to practice?

You are wise to recognize that practicing is the big stumbling block of the fledgling piano student. Some activities, such as learning crafts, may require no practice outside the lessons. Other activities, such as tumbling, require practice but can be done in the company of others. However, music lessons without practice are a waste of time and money. Furthermore, the practice must be done alone. It is solitary, not sociable. And the practice must be regular. Although the beginner's practice session might be brief, it must be held every day. A long session once or twice a week will not work. Here is how you can help your child.

1) Determine a regular time for practice. Many young children are worn out after a full day of school and are not able to tackle piano practice at three o'clock. Early evening is a possibility, although distraction from other family members and competition from homework and television pose problems. Early morning may be the best time for young children to practice. They are often early risers anyway, and they are rested and eager at this time. One full-time musician schedules all the lessons for his younger pupils before school. He finds they are freshest for lessons at seven or seven-thirty in the morning.

2) You will probably need to stay with your child for all or most of the practice sessions. It helps if you know a little about music. Even if you do not, however, you can help organize, often a difficult challenge for a young child.

Know what music has been assigned. See that he practices all his music. See that he goes over the difficult parts. Most children like to skip the hard parts and play what they already know well. Your task is to encourage him to practice the difficult parts. At the same time listen to the things he does well. The child gets pleasure and satisfaction from playing what he already knows. Help him balance the easy and the difficult.

3) Consider what outside incentives you might offer. Enthusiasm for music might be enough to motivate your child. After a while, however, treats and rewards might also help to provide an incentive. Food, money or a privilege might each be used as a reward. You might give a star for each practice. Four stars (four days) in a week merit a small treat; five stars, a medium treat; six stars, a big treat.

You can help your child by finding a regular time, helping with the practices and providing incentives. If you start lessons, continue long enough to give them a good try. Expect occasional grumpy days, but in general music should be fun.

If your child develops a real dislike for practicing, stop the lessons and introduce music in other ways. Select records which will expose him to music of all sorts at home. Consider the school band where most practicing can be done during school time. Or consider piano at a later age when your son is more mature and better able to structure his own time and practicing. The most important goal is not to make your child a great musician but to give him knowledge and a liking for the great gift of music.

23. Respect: How can we teach our children to respect us?

We have two children, a boy, age fourteen, and a girl, age twelve, who seem to have lost all respect for their dad and me. No matter what we say, they have a "smart" remark. Lately they shout back and call me names. How can I teach my children to respect us?

Thanks for a hard question, but a common one. Young adolescents are apt to express rebellion in words, which can be unpleasant.

This stage presents you with a difficult dilemma. You want your children to communicate with you, so you want to know their feelings. On the other hand, you know that one word often leads to another, and you would like to keep their negative feelings from getting out of hand.

At one extreme is the father who says (or shouts): "Don't ever let me hear you talk like that to your mother again!" Even if he is successful (and it may not work), the adolescent may take his command as a warning not to talk back at all. Then parents are deprived of learning their child's negative feelings.

Negative feelings are not nice. Adolescents have negative feelings when they feel restricted by family rules, when disciplined and simply when life goes awry. Parents do not have to give in when a child expresses resentment, but it might be wise to listen.

Often negative feelings are expressed in unacceptable ways, like shouting or defying. Part of good parenting is teaching children not to suppress angry feelings but to phrase them in acceptable words. Sometimes this practice takes a while to enact, but learning how to express resentment is much better than learning it must be kept inside.

The best way to learn proper expression of negative feelings is from parental example. Do you show your children respect? Are you able to express your own feelings in "I" statements, without blaming your spouse or children? Do you keep your own voice down and avoid inflammatory words?

If you do allow some negative expression, certain rules are obvious. Some words need to be outlawed, particularly obscene and swear words. Perhaps you can institute a small fine (ten cents) every time anyone raises his or her voice in anger or uses one of the "outlawed" words. Put the money in a "love" jar and contribute it to a worthy cause.

Another rule is no hitting. If the feuding degenerates to

hitting, then the combatants must be separated. It is best to do this firmly but without a lecture and blaming. Each party might go to a previously designated place.

Have a code word for such situations. Whenever anyone says the magic word (e.g., "Rumpelstiltskin"), the disputants must go to their agreed-upon places for at least sixty seconds.

At the same time, encourage the expression of gripes and resentments at regularly scheduled family meetings. Perhaps you can have a "free time" when people can speak their minds and pet peeves without interruption or blame.

The true measure of respect is whether children obey. Personally, I am willing to accept some appropriate back talk as long as children do what is required. The back talk keeps me informed of how they are feeling and is, thus, somewhat valuable.

Nevertheless, words can aggravate a situation. Be careful you don't shout back and try to get in the last word yourself. Instead, meet together at a calm moment and try to come up with a game plan for keeping back talk within bounds.

24. Running Away: How do you deal with teens who have run away?

Last week after my husband and I had an explosive session with our teenage daughter, she ran away from home. She literally packed a suitcase and took off. She was gone the entire night. We found her the next day staying at a friend's apartment and trying to find a ride out of town. I'm angry about this, yet I'm afraid she will do it again, so I don't know how to handle it. She is home now, for the moment anyway.

If you are like most parents, your runaway child has severely jolted your confidence in yourselves as parents. When your child runs away, you feel angry with your child and at the same time a total failure as a parent. Before you can deal with your daughter, therefore, you must deal with your own feelings about yourself as a parent.

The fact that your daughter ran away need not indicate that you are a failure as a parent. Other factors are at work here which you might reflect upon.

First, running away among teenage girls is on the increase. Since women have so many opportunities today and, at the same time, such confusion about the role of women, the teenage girl is in a particularly stressful situation. While she does not know just what being a woman entails, your daughter does know she can try daring, independent actions formerly reserved for boys— such as running away.

Second, not all pressures on teens come from home. Teens are beset with all kinds of pressures from school, peers, perhaps a job. When enough pressures build up they, like adults, sometimes just want to escape from a too painful situation. While a fight at home may have triggered the behavior, there are other factors in your daughter's life besides her home.

Third, as strange as it sounds, running away indicates some positive things about your daughter. A teenager must be a rather strong and independent person even to try running away. While strength and independence hardly seem like virtues when used against parents, they are actually necessary qualities for teens to develop if they are to cope with the world on their own within a year or two. Somehow you are raising a strong, independent daughter, and that part is good.

What you want to find out in dealing with your daughter is: Why did she run away? What is so difficult about life at home or her life outside her home? How can life at home be made more pleasant for you and her? How can you help her cope with her life in general?

Frequently after a crisis both parents and teen can be more open with their feelings about certain situations. This means you must express your own feelings about the incident. Telling your daughter she has been bad and must be punished tells her nothing about how you feel. It would probably lead to angry silence on her part. On the other hand, telling her how concerned you were when she was gone, how relieved you were to find her and how much you want to make home a happier place for all concerned is telling how you feel. Given this message, your daughter might tell you how she feels.

In regard to discipline, the parent of the runaway is tempted toward one of two extremes: either to be so severe she will never try that again or to be very lenient for fear she will run away again. Actually there is no way, either by force or by emotional pressure, that you can prevent your daughter from running away. If she wants to, it is easy. That is why it is so important to find out how she feels and what she wants and expects from her home life.

A behavior contract might help you through this stormy time in parent-teen relationships (see "Behavior Contracting" in Chapter Four). What behavior of hers is important to you: regular attendance at school, achieving certain grades, getting home on time, doing household chores? What rights or privileges does she want: later hours, permission to go places, use of the car?

In a behavior contract you spell out the demands that are important to you; she spells out the privileges that are important to her. By mutual agreement, when she meets your demands according to the contract, she gets the privilege she desires, also as spelled out in the contract.

The behavior contract helps parents and teens deal with an issue in a fairly factual manner at a time when emotion runs high on both sides. It helps both sides express what they really expect of each other. And it helps you to discipline in a reasonable manner at a time when it is easy to become too lenient or too severe.

25. Sex Education: What do you say to your children about sex?

I was dismayed when sex education was put into the school curriculum. Now they are even talking about condoms on radio and television. Worst of all, our pastor told us that we parents need to discuss sex in the home with our grade school children. I believe in letting sleeping dogs lie. I think this is wrong. Children so young are not ready for such information, and I won't have it in my home. Please comment.

Your pastor is wise. Parents need to let their children know that sex is not a taboo subject. Frankly, this cannot be done too soon today. The earlier the better. In a world which shouts its own jaded view of sex, we Christian parents are wrong to keep silent.

Silence is not golden. Rather, it is a dangerous cop-out, leaving the field clear for the carefree and exploitative commercialism of television, the crude messages on bathroom walls and misinformation of older youngsters. The question is not whether a child will receive a sex education too soon, but what kind of sex education he receives and who provides it.

Silence about sex is itself an education. The implicit message is clear: Sexual matters are to be kept secret. Or in so many unspoken parental words: "Don't talk to me about sex. I am uneasy discussing it, and I'd rather pretend it's not there."

Unfortunately, all that happens is that parents with this philosophy take themselves out of the picture. Even when children have a legitimate question or concern, they know better than to ask their parents. But do they remain totally uninformed about the issue? Hardly.

Curiosity is a powerful drive, even stronger than passion. Consider how many things dance through our minds within a short period of sixty seconds. Our minds are extremely active, hungry for sensation and information. Curiosity is the psychological counterpart of our physical sense of touch. It is vital to life.

More young people are led into premature sexual intercourse out of curiosity than passion. It is difficult to be passionate about something with which we have had no experience. Because curiosity is a major initial motivation for sex it is of the utmost importance that parents satisfy a child's curiosity. An honest verbal explanation is surely preferable to a premature blundering into a sexual experience.

Our eagerness to learn, our imagination, our hunger for stimulation all drive us to discover. Almost universally, preschool boys and girls will peek at one another's genitals or even show them openly to one another. Bodies are on display in *Playboy* and similar magazines. Just because they are not available in our home does not mean that our children will not see them.

More brazenly, television displays couples making out and making love. Here again, parents may forbid such viewing in their own home, but there is no way to protect a child from other children who have been thus educated and indoctrinated, or from bathroom walls at school with four-letter words and crude rhymes.

Wouldn't it be better if the "good guys" got there first? Whatever parents say, even if it is an awkward and stumbling admission of their discomfort, at least the child learns that sex is a subject that can be discussed with parents.

26. Shoplifting: Our son has been caught stealing from a store. What should we do?

Our ten-year-old son was caught shoplifting. We had to go to the police station to pick him up. He was crying, and frankly I don't know whether to be furious or feel sorry for him.

The police told us the store routinely presses charges and that we will have to make restitution and talk with the juvenile probation officer. Meanwhile, our son is not welcome in the store without a parent until the matter has been cleared up.

My husband and I are embarrassed. What should we do

now? Do you think the store owners and police are overreacting? He took about thirty dollars' worth of toy figures.

So far, everyone seems to have done well in responding. No, I do not think the store and police overreacted. The best way to stop shoplifting is to respond briefly but sternly to the first incident before it becomes a habit.

Unfortunately, shoplifting is all too common, not only among children but adults. The motivation for children is frequently the thrill of risk, to see if they can get away with it. Your son has received a clear message that he cannot. As a parent you should be pleased he was caught. In fact, a phone call to the store owner apologizing for your son and yourself and thanking him for handling it appropriately might be a nice gesture.

The next steps are very important. First, come down sternly. Your son needs to understand that his parents and the community take shoplifting seriously. The store management and the police may already have sent this message. So do not try to make excuses for your son because of his age and his tears. In fact, you may add your own statement: "Don't ever do this again. We Smiths do not steal from stores or other people."

Second, set the penalty and get it over with. A specific number of hours of hard work such as housecleaning or yard cleanup until restitution is made would be one good idea. Payment for thirty dollars' worth of merchandise demands more than a token job. Ten hours of work might be appropriate. Denying television until the work is completed would be reasonable. This manual labor allows your son to respond to his misdeed by doing something worthwhile. He needs to know that although he has done something bad, he himself is a good person.

A long lecture on the folly or immorality of shoplifting would not be wise, nor would a punishment that lasted for weeks. The reason for keeping punishment brief is to give as little attention as possible to the behavior (shoplifting) you wish to stop. Long punishments have the unfortunate consequence of providing secondary gain, that is, they give too much attention to the misbehavior.

It is probably a mistake for you and your son to see the probation officer over a period of time. Tell the probation officer how you handled the problem within the family. If you do, one visit to the probation officer should be enough.

Third, let your son know that, although everyone makes mistakes, you love him. A hug following your brief, stern lecture is a good start in this direction.

Don't be embarrassed. This problem occurs frequently. You now have an opportunity for some good parenting. Be stern. Be brief. And then be positive.

27. Shyness: How can I help my son with his shyness?

My six-year-old son embarrasses us in public. He doesn't throw temper tantrums. In fact, he behaves just the opposite. He acts shy. When I try to introduce him to a friend, he hides behind me, clings to me or even crawls under the table. Then in a few minutes, he starts acting foolishly, making funny faces or noises, or doing minor nuisance things to get attention. Why can't he behave properly? We have taught him the right manners.

The behavior you describe so well is rather typical for a six-year-old. Like the adolescent in our culture, the six-year-old is in transition, making his first major break from the home. He goes off to school and out to play. Home may remain a safe harbor, but he surely does not spend all his time there.

Also like the adolescent, the six-year-old is ambivalent about his entry into the world outside the home. One day he will want to be away from the family; the next day he may cling like a frightened two-year-old. He reaches out and pulls back. For a while his double role might cause much parental consternation.

What can you do? First, you can ignore the shy behavior. Don't force him to be polite, mannerly and outgoing. Allow him to progress at his own rate. As you say, he may well know the proper social behavior. That does not mean, however, that he finds it easy to observe.

A second thing you can do is polish your own social graces. Let your son observe you greeting people properly and warmly with a smile, hello and handshake. Parental example will be the best teacher in the long run.

You mention that minor naughtiness follows his initial shy and awkward behavior. That, too, is very common.

The best thing to do here is to anticipate his need for attention. Rather than wait and have him force you to pay attention to his nuisance behavior, you might beat him at his own game with an early payoff for good behavior.

When your son goes into his shy, awkward act, look for something nice to reward with your attention. Perhaps his hair is combed, his shoes are tied, he has a smile on his face.

If he is not doing anything praiseworthy, then respond in other ways. Touch him. Tousle his hair. Call him by name.

Finally, if you wish him to be mannerly in public, then you and your husband should break down mannerliness into its smaller parts. The greeting ritual, for example, includes a smile, a touch, a hello and introductions.

Don't wait for all these to occur. Notice any one of them. Touch him when he smiles. Tell him that you're glad he shook hands.

This type of reinforcement is known as "shaping." Reward the bits and pieces. Eventually you will get the big picture.

The best thing you can do is to relax and be patient. I don't think we should force six-year-olds to know all the social skills at the very beginning of their social lives. Let them cling now and then if they need to do so. With parental example and support, most children will practice at least minimal social graces in a year or two.

28. Sibling Rivalry: How can I keep my children from fighting?

I have three daughters, one age seven and twins age four. The twins constantly whine over every little thing. If one looks at the other wrong, there's a fight. My oldest daughter picks a lot. I send to her room, which she argues about and won't budge, so I try to carry her and she throws a fit. I put the two girls in chairs because they share a room.

My husband works a swing shift so most of their upbringing is put on me. What am I doing wrong? I'm trying to be a good mother. I'm tired of yelling and losing my patience. Help!

Welcome to the real world. While the amount of fighting that occurs among children varies, fighting among brothers and sisters is almost universal. My purely subjective opinion is that there is even more "picking" between girls and most of all between girls who are close in age. To summarize, the situation you describe is normal. Fighting does not mean you are a bad mother or that you have bad children.

Notice two important facts about children's fussing relationships. First, children do not fight like adults. They do not carry grudges or hold deep anger. They are more like firecrackers—loud and fiery one moment, then completely over the outburst the next moment. (Of course another argument may erupt a few minutes later.)

Adults assume fighting children harbor the heavy feelings which adults do. They don't. Children's fighting is often intense. It is also superficial.

Since children's arguments are so heated, adults tend to see only the bad parts of the children's relationships and overlook the good parts. Paradoxically, those children who fight most frequently are often closest to each other emotionally. Look for positive elements.

Notice the good things your girls do. Even little remarks such as, "You set the table nicely tonight" or "You poured that milk very well" can set a positive tone.

Touch and hug your children frequently. If you are not used to doing so, remind yourself. Nothing does more to enhance a child's well-being and create a happy atmosphere.

Hungry, tired children fight more than rested, satisfied children. See that your children get meals and snacks at regular intervals and that regular bedtimes are observed. You will avoid many problem situations.

Now, here are two approaches which may help you cope with the actual fighting. First, try physical discipline. By physical I mean nonverbal. Separate the two of them.

You may want to prepare your response in advance. Define the problem concretely. Identify the words that inflame like "stupid," "jerk" and "weirdo." Rule out yelling and hitting. Then pinpoint the times that these words and behaviors occur. Talk with your husband about the most common times for combat. Let Dad go off with one of them and Mom with the other. That way they both get attention, and you have successfully disciplined the fighting by making it impossible. Children cannot fuss and fight if they are out of shouting distance.

If your husband is not home at the time of the fight, talk with a friend who has a similar problem. Enlist his or her help to diffuse the situation.

Suppose you are too late: The battle has already erupted. I would still separate them. Send one outside or to the other room. Do not try to intervene or settle the dispute fairly. Simply stop it by putting distance between them.

A second approach would be to reward non-fighting, to notice the children's quiet times and their good times together. Too often we parents get into the bad habit of responding only to misbehavior. We are silent when good things are going on.

Here again, use the charting techniques I discuss in Chapter Four to help change their behavior. Set up a simple chart with a space for each half hour. Give a smile face for each trouble-free period and an X when the fighting occurs. Responding with smile faces will remind you to notice when the good behavior occurs. While this effort may seem troublesome and a bit juvenile, it is surely better than not noticing and is an improvement over your present condition.

Remember, you are facing a problem which is as common as rain. Be patient. You can be successful.

29. Spoiling: Can you spoil a baby?

When my baby cries, I pick her up. I hold her a great deal, and some people say I'm spoiling her. Am I?

You're caught in the middle of an age-old dilemma—to let baby cry or to pick her up. I am one hundred percent on your side. Pick up your baby. I think you'll understand why if you look at the nature of infants.

The first clue that crying is not good for babies is that crying bothers us. The sound of infant crying upsets any human being, male or female, big or little. Since this reaction is universal, I think we can justly interpret it as a natural signal: "This baby needs something. Do something." If you need further convincing that crying bothers us, observe older children. An adult might put off a crying baby, even claim crying is "good" for the baby. A child never will. A child quickly and insistently announces to the mother, "The baby's crying!"

Perhaps one reason we adults feel we should put off a crying baby is that we see crying as bad behavior. That is what your critics mean when they say "Let your baby cry or you'll spoil her." Crying is bad only from the adult viewpoint. From the baby's viewpoint crying is communication. Books, workshops and therapy sessions abound to teach people how to communicate. It seems inconsistent to ignore this very little person's efforts to communicate.

Does holding spoil babies? Again we look to nature for the answer. Almost everyone has observed young puppies or kittens. They snuggle close to their litter mates and stay with the mother almost constantly. Separation from mother

171

and siblings is the ultimate in distress. In the animal kingdom it seems almost universal that newborns need mother, not occasionally, not when she has time for them, not on a four-hour schedule, but almost constantly. Why do we think that human babies should be happy alone in a large crib in a private room? When your baby asks to be held and snuggled, she is demonstrating the new baby's need for warmth, cuddling and human contact. This need exists more or less on a twenty-four hour basis.

Your baby needs to be held, touched. The skin is an organ. Research suggests that skin stimulation is not simply a nice extra between mother and baby, but a need as vital as food and warmth. So hold, touch, stroke, enjoy.

Of course this does not mean a mother ought to do nothing but hold her baby twenty-four hours a day. Comforting a new baby is not as impossible as it sounds. The younger the baby, the greater the need to be held. This fits in beautifully with the mother's own need. In the early days and weeks after birth, she spends the most time with her baby. This is the time when she can and *should* have an easy work schedule to relax and enjoy her baby. If she is tired, she can crawl into bed with baby to rest or nap. After all, a baby snuggled close to Mom will usually oblige by dropping off to sleep.

As the baby grows, he still needs his mother but less constantly. Daddy and other soothing, loving relatives and friends make wonderful baby holders. Slings and carriers enable Mom to fasten baby on her. Carriers are indispensable for walking, shopping or for use around the house. Baby nestles close to Mom in utmost contentment, and Mom has a free hand to do what needs to be done.

As the weeks pass, baby becomes increasingly aware of her surroundings. She then enjoys short periods in an infant seat, preferably in the center of the household where she can watch the action. When she has had enough and wants cuddling or sleep, she will let you know.

When a child reaches eighteen months or two years, we begin to have certain expectations and make certain demands on her. Then it is quite possible to spoil. But now we are talking about babies, and babies are to love. The time when baby needs Mom all the time is actually very short. Enjoy your baby. You can't spoil a baby by giving her what she needs. You might, however, spoil a baby by *not* giving her what she needs.

30. Suicide: Will my daughter try suicide again?

My seventeen-year-old daughter tried to end her life. She came into my bedroom and showed me an empty bottle of sleeping pills she purchased herself and without prescription at our local drugstore. She told me she had taken all of them about a half hour earlier.

I rushed her to the hospital. For a while we did not know if she would live or die.

The following day she told me she didn't want to live because her boyfriend had begun to flirt with other girls. She felt she was a failure in school and wanted to get away from having to decide what to do when she graduates.

She and her boyfriend have made up, but her dad and I still feel uneasy. Is there something we should be doing to prevent a recurrence?

You are correct to be concerned. Suicide is the second leading cause of death in the teen and young-adult age groups, right behind automobile accidents.

You acted quickly and wisely in taking your daughter to the hospital. If there is any question whether a lethal dose has been taken, the stomach should be emptied as soon as possible and certainly within one hour after the overdose.

The next step may be obvious, but too soon forgotten. I would clean out your daughter's room and dresser drawers of any tranquilizers, diet pills, other pills or sharp instruments. You can be quite open about this action, and she may object, but it is a sensible precaution.

After a suicide attempt, it is wise to see that the person has company for the next week or so. The companionship is not necessarily to generate communication or deep talks, but a rather obvious preventive.

I would try to eliminate your daughter's alcohol consumption during this period. Alcohol is a depressant. On top of an already existing blue mood, alcohol can intensify feelings of hopelessness.

You say you feel uneasy around her now. I understand that, but you must not pussyfoot. She is not a hothouse plant. If you treat her like one, she will feel demeaned.

Be direct and adult with her. Suicide cannot be a taboo topic. If you are concerned she might make another attempt, address this concern directly with her. Ask her if she plans to take her life. Don't be afraid to continue your usual discipline in other areas.

Your daughter might try to use the threat of suicide to get her way.

"I need to stay out extra late tonight. I have to talk with my friends because I feel depressed and I want to die, and you don't even care."

In such cases, try to treat the curfew issue objectively, while ignoring her thinly-veiled threats.

Finally, your daughter needs to see a psychologist or social worker at this time to address such issues as her self-image, her career plans, her relationship with her boyfriend and her thoughts about death. While family is important and your family may be close, your daughter may need the perspective of a trained outsider.

Throughout all of this, continue to be supportive and accepting of your daughter as she goes through a very difficult time.

31. Teenage Drinking: What's the best way to handle teen drinking?

Last weekend my seventeen-year-old came home drunk at three o'clock in the morning. He has never stayed out that late before, and he has never given us any trouble. The boys he pals around with seem to be nice boys. How should I handle him? What if it happens again?

According to the laws in our society, seventeen-year-olds may not drink. The simplest solution may seem to be to follow the laws, forbid your son to drink and punish him severely for drinking.

While this solution seems simple, I do not advise it for several reasons. First, you cannot enforce such a rule with a seventeen-year-old. He and his friends can drive; they have access to cars. If they choose, they can get away from all adult supervision and drink. You can enforce such a rule even less with an eighteen-year-old.

One of the main jobs of parenthood is to prepare a child for independence. In this case, parents have the right and duty to teach a child about alcohol and drinking behavior. If he is going to learn to drink and make some mistakes in the process, it is far better he do so while he is at home than after he leaves home as an adult. Teaching a child how to use alcohol is far more difficult than forbidding it, but it is the only approach which will help him in the next few years and throughout life.

In regard to last week's episode, listen to your son. Try to find out what happened, whom he was with, where and how much he drank. If you explode in anger or set down punishments immediately, you will cut off all further communication.

Tell your son how you feel. Do you feel all drinking is wrong? Do you feel drinking is all right at times, but getting drunk is unacceptable? Try to share your own views and feelings.

Try to talk about some of the problems he faces as a teenager. Does he know how to drink one drink slowly so that he consumes very little over a period of time? How might he handle peer pressure when he is with a group of boys for whom being one of the crowd means getting drunk? You cannot answer these questions easily any more than your son can, but if you can talk together about them, you can help him clarify his own thinking.

Finally, formulate some guidelines regarding drinking. For example, here are the ones my wife and I use with our teens:

1) *Never drive when you drink.* If you drink even one beer, call your parents for a ride home. It might be embarrassing, but it will keep you alive.

2) *No beer or liquor in the car.* Period. (For us, drinking and driving is the number one prohibition. Getting drunk won't kill you. Getting drunk and driving can kill you and some innocent motorist you hit.)

3) *Set limits on how much you can drink,* for example, three beers. Keep track after the first drink. There is no point in trying to count after you are too fuzzy to remember. Trust your limits and stick to them. Do not think you can add a few more because you don't seem to feel anything from what you have drunk so far.

4) *You may drink at home.* Your friends may drink at our house provided we have talked with their parents and their parents know and approve. Your friends may not drive afterwards. They may stay all night at our house or we will drive them home. Drinking with friends applies to an occasional weekend evening and a modest amount. We are not talking about a daily occurrence or about getting drunk.

5) *Coming home drunk will carry a penalty* spelled out in advance.

If you still have a problem with your teen drinking, try these two approaches.

If your teen continues to drink outside the home, then take away his car keys and/or car privileges.

Second, you may find it easier to focus on curfew rather than alcohol consumption. Arguing with your teen whether he has been drinking or not can be futile. If you discover your teen has been drinking, set a curfew of ten o'clock or even nine o'clock. Most teen drinking takes place after ten o'clock at night. Curfew is far easier to control than drinking.

Will these guidelines make your son a wise, sensible drinker? They will help. Growing up is rough, and there are setbacks. He may come home drunk again, and you will have to enforce whatever penalty you have established. The importance of setting guidelines is to spell out clearly what is acceptable and what is not. Persons who have learned how to handle alcohol are less apt to become alcohol abusers. Guidelines help him chart a path in dealing with a new situation: drinking behavior.

32. Teenage Driving: How can we set teenage driving privileges?

Our sixteen-year-old son will be getting his driver's license soon. I would like some suggestions about letting him use the family car. We have only one car, and we will have three drivers—my husband, myself and our son.

Parents hold widely differing policies in regard to driving privileges for teens. Some parents never permit their children to drive the family car. If you want to drive, they say, earn and finance your own car. Other parents grant unlimited use of the family car or even buy a car for the child. Most parents fall somewhere between these two extremes.

The amount you let your son use the car is up to you. There is no right answer. You will probably maintain a smoother relationship, however, if you spell out the policies early in his driving career.

Assuming you are going to share the family car, here are some points you need to consider.

Who pays for insurance? Insuring a teenage male is expensive. Your insurance company can quote you a rate and tell you how much of the total cost is from having a teenage male driver in the family.

Who pays for gas? When this policy is not spelled out, frequently everyone involved feels cheated. Your son thinks he puts in more than his share and Dad feels he is always filling the empty tank that his son left him. If this issue causes controversy, you can try a weekly assessment for your son or he can keep track of the miles he drives.

How often can he have the car? If this issue is not spelled out, your son might have to depend on your mood. When you feel good, he can have the car; if not, he can't. Such uncertainty can make him resentful and frustrated. You might agree he can have the car one night per week or whenever he gives you a day's notice. Obviously, emergencies and family needs supersede his claim, but having a policy can avoid a lot of resentment.

Where can he go? Must he let you know where he is taking the car? May he leave town? Must he let you know he is leaving town? Such questions arise in a mobile culture such as ours.

What about drinking and driving? Are there special penalties for this very serious offense? (See Question 31.)

There are some problems to anticipate: Who pays in the event of an accident? Who pays if he gets a ticket? Are there any penalties from you for getting a ticket or for getting stopped by the police?

Will taking away the use of the car ever be used as a punishment? If so, will this punishment be used for any offense or only for abuse of driving privileges?

Asking all these questions may seem to be making too much of a simple privilege. However common it may be in our country, driving a car *is* a privilege involving a lot of money and a lot of responsibility. Anticipating the problems and talking them over with your son can alleviate many controversies and misunderstandings.

33. Teens: How can a parent like and enjoy teenagers?

My two teens are so self-centered. They are never around for meals or work but always there to ask for money. And they can't make up their minds. One minute they are so sure they want to do something; the next minute, they're just the opposite. I keep telling myself that it's just a stage, but then I get terrified: What if they stay like this? More to the point, I want to like and enjoy my teens. How can I?

The teenage years are difficult times, but they are exciting as well. I don't know if you can enjoy your teens. I am sure, however, that they can add spice to your life.

Teen years are an in-between time. On the one hand, youngsters are pulling at the reins, trying to break free. In an immature attempt to demonstrate their adulthood, they may break every household rule.

On the other hand, they are scared. Despite their need to break out, they do not have a partner or career of their own. They are rebelling against their family of childhood without having the security of a replacement or the status of a career.

For these reasons, the teen years pose an identity crisis. Not content with the status of unemployed child, the teen strains to break free. It is the parents' privilege (or problem) to try to hold all the pieces together while the teen finds out who he or she is and what life is all about.

Teens are not the only ones to be scared. Parents get scared, too. Parents can see all the dangers inherent in trying one's wings: cars that go too fast, sex that leads to pregnancy, drugs and alcohol that can steal a mind and warp behavior. The price of a mistake may seem too high for a parent to tolerate. Hence, many parents tighten controls and enforce strict obedience.

On the other hand, teens must have room to grow. If independence is the goal (and it is), strict obedience is not a good prelude to complete freedom. There must be a more gradual loosening of the reins. It's true: If you give them room to grow, teens will add spice to your life as well as gray to your hair. But you must take some risks. You must also be there to applaud them when efforts go well, and even more, to support them when they stumble.

Let them gain some life experience while living at home, before going away to college or moving into their own homes. You should be available when they make their first big mistakes.

Parents of teens are caught between two difficult choices. If you set up multiple rules and enforce total obedience, teens will not be prepared to make choices on their own when they leave. On the other hand, if you have no rules, teens may run wild and destroy themselves. You need considerable wisdom to strike a middle path.

The best answer may be to impose some general rules without filling in all the details. Curfew and driving behavior are two good areas to address. Use common sense. Let them drive, but if they drink or speed, take away the keys for a month. Let them date, but see that they are home at a reasonable hour. Let them drink a beer or glass of wine at home, but if they come home drunk, enforce a strict curfew.

Stick to these rules and give them some freedom in other areas. Then watch and pray.

34. Television: What should children watch on TV?

I try to police my children's TV watching. So far I've forbidden TV programs with violence, glorified sex and family-situation comedies that make a farce of family life. About the only thing left that my kids like besides sports are the game shows like The Price Is Right *and* Let's Make a Deal. *What do you think?*

Good for you! I am glad someone is concerned about the quantity and the content of TV watching by our children. I think the game shows, however, are the most dangerous of all TV programs for our children. They glorify the twin evils of our times: materialism and personal competition.

With all the other types of programs, the problems you mention are overt. It is easier for a parent to counteract or forbid when the issue is obvious. Violence, inappropriate sex and making fun of the family can all be identified and either commented on or turned off.

Materialism, however, is not so easy. Greed is insidious in our culture. Advertising repetitively urges us to "Buy, buy, buy!" Overconsumption becomes an accepted part of our daily life. Emphasis on self and the accumulation of material goods that please the self can become the primary concern of our lives.

All that is worst about materialism is present in the TV game shows. Things are glorified. The clear message is that material goods make a person happy.

Game shows feature mostly luxury items. They attempt to create new desires in the viewers and to turn these desires into needs. Suddenly we need things we never even knew existed.

Finally, game shows promote person-against-person competition. One contestant's gain is another's loss. Unfortunately, much of our society operates on that basis. We have enough victory and defeat in our society; we do not need to compound it in our entertainment. I can do without unnecessary competition. I can find other ways to be with my "brothers and sisters" than trying to beat them at something.

There are several things you as a concerned parent might do. First, limit TV time. I think two hours of TV viewing per day are plenty. To avoid viewing simply to kill time, family members might select certain programs from a TV guide each week, then forget about the rest.

Second, you may wish to forbid certain programs you find offensive to taste or morals.

Third, watch television with your children. Point out the problems and the things that upset you. You may wish to comment, for example, on game shows that are ninety percent advertising.

Fourth, model and teach good behavior away from the TV set, for example, by practicing rational buying and consumption yourself.

35. Temper Tantrums: What should I do when my child has a temper tantrum?

My four-year-old likes to have temper tantrums when he knows I can't control him. Yesterday, in the toy department of a large store, he had a perfect kicking and screaming fit when I wouldn't buy him what he wanted. He will do this at home, too, but not as often. Mostly he puts on his show when I'm in a public place and I get very embarrassed.

I feel a child should definitely be spanked within the framework of love and affection.

Temper tantrums are common among preschool children. It is our job as parents to teach our children some self-control. I have some general common sense rules about temper tantrums which may be of some help.

1) For your own sake, avoid letting the tantrum occur in public places. If your child is prone to tantrums while shopping, then don't take him shopping. Get a babysitter or leave him with a friend. If he does begin to carry on in a public place, pick him up and take him out to the car. Don't stay around to get embarrassed and then angry at him. Remove him from the scene.

2) Don't give in. It is important not to reward the unwanted behavior. You can be patient and let his anger run its course, but don't give him what he wants.

3) Protect him, yourself and anybody and anything else from harm. Move him to a place where he can kick and thrash around without hurting anyone—or embarrassing you.

4) It is probably wise to avoid physical punishment. Some parents claim that a slap or a glass of cold water will shock a child out of a particular behavior. I am more inclined to let the temper run its course without any reward.

5) Ignore the tantrum as much as you can. Get him to a safe

place. Protect everyone. Then let him unwind. Ignoring is more effective than punishing in the long run. Punishment can sometimes stop a behavior right now. But by ignoring you have a better chance to get rid of bad behavior for good.

6) Pay attention to other worthwhile behavior. If you can, try to distract him during the tantrum. Get him interested in doing something else. If not, wait until the tantrum is over and then get him involved in a worthwhile activity. This practice is far more effective than a lecture from you on why tantrums are not nice. It is better to teach your child what to do than what not to do.

There are two kinds of temper tantrums, or rather there is a continuum between two poles. On one side is the con job, where the child rather calculatingly throws a tantrum to get his way. On the other side, there is berserk behavior, where the child has clearly lost control. The situation you refer to was of the con job type.

With a con job tantrum, once the child is safe from harm and the parent safe from embarrassment, it is wisest to ignore the misbehavior. The child soon learns this is not an effective way to accomplish his goal. It doesn't work. Eventually, he will try some other way and the parent begins to pay attention again.

The situation is different with a berserk tantrum. The child has lost control of his own behavior and is flailing around, the helpless victim of his own rage. It would be cruel to let this kind of behavior go on for long. The object is to get through to the child in whatever way works. You might pick him up and hold him, insist he sit in a certain spot, show him an unusual object. The purpose is not to punish the child but rather to interrupt a rage that is out of control. Only then can the rage be managed. You must try different techniques to find out what is most effective. Strange as it sounds, a two-year-old might respond to a command to sit on a kitchen stool. The out-of-control rage is then diverted to an action.

The important thing is to control behavior. When you say the child has defied authority and must be spanked to indicate to him that you can control him, I think you are being one-dimensional. You are operating solely in the authoritative dimension. There are other ways to influence and change the actions of our children.

I am not advocating permissiveness; children's behavior often needs set boundaries. I am saying quite simply that these boundaries do not always need to be set by edict or punishment. Behavior can be shaped in many ways.

36. Toilet Training: What is the easiest way to toilet train?

My only child is just two years old. He is not yet toilet trained. I want to train him in the easiest way. Some of my friends have been at it for months, and they are very frustrated. I don't want this to happen to me.

You have pinpointed the most essential element of successful toilet training: It is a normal learning experience for the growing child. Don't ever let it become a frustration for either of you.

Two conditions can keep toilet training simple. First, be sure the child is ready. Second, train the easy way.

I suggest five ways to determine readiness.

1) Your child must be walking for some months before he is physically developed enough to be toilet trained.

2) Occasionally you should also find your child dry after a two- or three-hour stretch. Extended periods of dryness indicate your child has some control over urination.

3) Since communication is a part of toilet training, it helps if your child is able to talk a bit.

4) Your child often goes through an ornery period when "no" is the favorite word. Common sense suggests you

delay toilet training until such a period abates somewhat.

5) Finally, toilet training should be postponed when your child has a new brother or sister, has just come home from the hospital or when another life crisis has just occurred in your child's life.

Taken together these factors indicate that your child will probably be ready for toilet training sometime between the ages of two and three. Until that time do nothing about toilet training.

Once your child is ready, try this easy way to train him in one week. Choose a consecutive five-day period (e.g., Monday through Friday) when both you and your child are feeling good and you have few other obligations. Put a child's potty in a room with a hard floor covering (let's be practical) where you plan to spend the morning. Remove your son's diaper, socks and shoes and let him run freely. Give him water and juice liberally, and wait for nature. When he starts to go or indicates he has to go, scoop him up gently and put him on the potty. Ignore any misses on the floor and praise and reward anything that gets in the potty.

One half day is long enough to be vigilant. In the afternoon put diapers back on him and relax. Do the same thing each morning. By Thursday or Friday your son should be catching on. If so, continue extending the time he goes without diapers, and praise and reward all his successes.

If your son is not catching on or if either of you is getting frustrated, quit. Wait a couple of months and try again. If a child is not toilet trained within five days, the cost in anxiety and frustration outweighs the benefit.

There is no harm in postponing toilet training for a few weeks or months. There can be great harm in making it a heavy issue between you and your child. So toilet train the easy way both for your sake and that of your child.

37. Vacations: Should we force our teens to come along on vacation?

Now that our two oldest children are teens, they no longer want to come along on family vacations. Should we arrange to have them stay home or force them to come along in the hope we will have a good time once we're on the road?

Parents are apt to be baffled about how to handle the question of family vacations unless they remember two important things about teens. First, the influence of friends is all-important. Therefore, while parents look forward to getting away from the daily routines, teens fear they will miss something. "If I leave," your daughter is thinking, "Susie will find another best friend while I'm gone."

Second, teens tend to distrust their parents' taste. Therefore, while parents look forward to new experiences and new locations, teens suspect that whatever parents plan will be boring. A worse fate cannot be imagined: to be stuck in your parents' company *and* to be bored.

Once parents recognize these facts about teen behavior, a family vacation is not only possible but potentially satisfying. The first step is to choose a vacation that offers something for everyone. What does your family like to do on vacation? Do you want to cover a lot of miles and see and do a lot in a short time or do you want to relax, unwind and get away from the daily pressure? Getting away outdoors, whether camping or in a cabin, remains universally popular because fishing, water sports, hiking and campfires can be enjoyed by all ages.

Here are some questions teens often raise about vacations:

1) *"May I bring a friend?"* Once the vacation has been established, this is usually the next question. While it may be impossible in terms of space, this is not an unreasonable request. An only girl in a family of boys might enjoy the vacation much more if she is allowed to bring a girlfriend. Having a companion might draw the

teen away from the family but, on the other hand, both might be drawn into family activities. At any rate it should improve the vacation for the child involved.

2) *"How long will we be gone?"* If teens are reluctant, a maximum of one week is a good idea. The time can be sandwiched between school and summer jobs. This allows time for the family to get away together and still not interfere seriously with individual plans.

3) *"Do I have to babysit the little ones?"* When there is a wide age spread in the family, teens enjoy their younger brothers and sisters for short periods, but they are dubious about twenty-four-hour-a-day togetherness. On a camping vacation our teens appreciate having a car available and being able to investigate the nearest city on their own—not every night, just once or twice. On other nights the campfire is more appealing because they know they aren't forced to be there.

4) *"Do I have to go along?"* My wife and I do not like to force teens (or anyone else) to do things. But in this case, we *force*. If parents really include everyone in the choice of a vacation, keep it short enough not to interfere with other plans and permit teens some freedom of movement, the teens are likely to enjoy it despite some initial grumbling. A vacation provides a unique situation for families to get reacquainted away from individual routines. This is an opportunity too good to miss.

38. War Toys: Should children play with guns?

My son will celebrate his tenth birthday soon and is talking about presents he would like. Everything on his list involves soldiers, guns and warfare. My husband and I are sensitive to the violence in society. I don't know where his attraction to war figures comes from and I don't want to encourage it. Any suggestions?

An enterprising student could write a cultural history of our country based on the changing taste in children's toys over the years. War toys were extremely popular during the early 1960s. As opposition to involvement in Vietnam and sensitivity to violence in society grew, war toys fell out of favor. As we have moved into the 1990's, war toys are again on the ascendancy.

Often television is blamed. Like most easy answers, blaming television is inadequate. While television cannot explain an interest in war toys, it certainly capitalizes on this interest by promoting war in stories and cartoons, and by selling war toys through commercials. Dealing with this emphasis requires your parental effort. Forbidding television or condemning your child's choice of programs often makes the forbidden item more attractive. While you might limit your child's viewing hours, counteracting television demands that you find other activities to replace it.

Encourage your son to invite his friends over after school. Having several children around for snacks and playtime will require extra effort, but it will also get your children away from the after-school cartoons. If they sit in front of the TV screen, get them interested in something else.

Schedule a trip with your son to a toy store. Although he may head straight for the war toys, other toys will undoubtedly catch his eye. Attractive new toys will also catch your eye. Find out what other toys seem to interest him. Find something better than a war toy for his birthday. Ten-year-olds often like sets with many figures and parts. Electronic toys, the kind that move and make noise and require lots of batteries, are frequently poor toys because they are cheaply made and break down easily. On the other hand, most ten-year-olds are enchanted by movement, lights and beepers. A pocket calculator or pocket electronic game might be welcome.

Ten-year-olds are just approaching the age when sports equipment and sports clothing are welcome. Special shoes, warm-up suits and sports equipment are possibilities.

Do not overlook your own special interests. Ten-year-olds can begin to share activities with their parents. If you enjoy a hobby such as photography or fishing, you might buy your son some equipment for a beginner in this field.

Talk to other parents. You are not the only parent disturbed by war toys. Pool ideas. If other children do not have war toys, they will diminish in importance. Persons concerned about violence have formed local and national groups. You might join such a group to gain support, to promote ideas and to join others in finding ways to raise your family in a less violent climate.

Personally, I would not forbid a child to buy war toys with his own money. Forbidding only makes the item doubly attractive and causes arguments. And given the cost of toys and the limited resources of most ten-year-olds, his purchases will be few.

But, like you, I would not betray my beliefs by purchasing war toys as gifts. If parents and grandparents refuse to purchase them, war toys will soon disappear from the market.